A Country Where All Colors
Are Sacred and Alive

A Memoir of Non-Ordinary Experience
and Collaboration with Nature

Geoffrey Oelsner

Lorian Press
Everett, Washington

A Country Where All Colors Are Sacred and Alive

A Memoir of Non-Ordinary Experience and Collaboration with Nature

by Geoffrey Oelsner

Eckhart Tolle quoted from Stillness Speaks, Vancouver, Canada, Namaste Publishing, 2003, pp. 84-86, with the kind permission of Namaste Publishing.

Cover painting: "Scott Creek Afternoon" by Robert Sudlow
Photograph of Geoffrey Oelsner by Richard Berquist

Cover and interior design: Joy Caffrey
Design assistance and prepress production: Jeremy Berg

Published by Lorian Press
2204 E. Grand Ave.
Everett, WA 98201
www.lorian.org

ISBN: 978-0-936878-41-6

First Edition: February, 2012
Printed in the United States of America
9 8 7 6 5 4 3 2 1 0

I dedicate this book to

Dorothy Maclean,
co-founder of the Findhorn Community,

the late Robert Sudlow,
Kansas landscape artist,

and to everyone who contributes to harmony
between Humanity and Nature

Love and gratitude to my spiritual friends

Sandra Glickman, David Spangler, Anna Cox,

and to my beloved partner Leslie

Contents

List of Illustrations

Author's note: The word "nature" is capitalized throughout this book, to emphasize Nature's seamless oneness with Spirit, God, Goddess, or whatever word we may use to denote that Sacred Mystery.

Sacred Exchanges with Nature
(An Overview)

Many of us have experiences that point toward a more holistic, interconnected Reality than we normally perceive. Episodes of telepathy, spontaneous healings, confirmed intuitions, precognition, attunement to nonphysical beings, nonlocal awareness, or communion with the natural world--all these can expand our understanding of what is possible for us and remind us of an undivided spiritual dimension of ourselves.

This memoir in prose and poetry is an account of my continuing education in such experiences, which can make us more aware of that dimension of oneness, and empower us to step forward into more conscious, collaborative relationships with the sentient energies of Nature. These sacred relationships can contribute to environmental harmony right now, and may help downscale our climatic predicament in days to come.

This book originated from a sermon which I delivered to the Unitarian Universalist Fellowship in my home town. Titled "Sacred Exchanges with Nature," the sermon set forth a vision of our intimacy with Nature, and offered scientific evidence as well as personal anecdotes supportive of the thesis that we can nurture the natural world through meditation, prayer, blessing, positive intention, loving presence, mindful ritual, celebration, song, dance, and other expressions of joyful creativity.

In the frightening face of all we read and observe about climate change, this is an important and heartening message: yes, political and grassroots action is absolutely essential for the protection of our environment, but so is what American spiritual teacher and author David Spangler calls "subtle activism."

I have actively addressed community health and environmental issues for thirty-five years now. I've worked as a community organizer in Georgia and Arkansas, engaged with others in anti-nuclear research and activism, co-authored a book about natural forms of radiation protection, and most recently have joined the growing number of people working to alert the public and public health officials to the environmental hazards of "fracking" for

1

subterranean natural gas deposits. I am convinced that we can help sustain and restore environmental harmony through our loving interactions with the natural world in a way that complements such necessary political work.

In the course of presenting "Sacred Exchanges with Nature" to my Unitarian friends, I shared two personal stories about dramatic interactions with natural forces which happened to me in the presence of other observers, further opening my eyes to our inherent oneness with Nature. I was initially concerned that these stories might be too far out, way too woo-woo for a cognitively-oriented crowd of Unitarians skeptical about things mystical and parapsychological. However, my listeners seemed to take the two unusual tales I shared in stride, along with the rest of the sermon, and afterwords I felt encouraged to continue to share them in an interactive workshop.

I also began to wonder how many similar non-ordinary experiences I'd had which could be confirmed by subsequent events, or verified by the observations of others who were present with me, or which were otherwise not strictly subjective, but at least partially founded in tangible, external phenomena. I decided to compile a chronological memoir of such experiences, supplementing them with relevant anecdotes and reflections.

Over a period of about a year, I primed the pump of my memory and collected a journal full of such stories, to which I added a number of others about off-the-chart synchronicities and instances of what some researchers into the anomalous call "High Strangeness." Certain vivid experiences of energies sensed in wilderness, or at ancient ceremonial and burial sites, got grandfathered in, though decidedly more subjective in character than other tales. Several unusual incidents occurred over the year which I appended to this collection, and here and there I threw in an original poem or song lyric which called for inclusion.

Gradually, a kind of patchwork parapsychological-autobiographical quilt emerged. (All of my recorded songs and some recordings of my poetry can be accessed for free at www.geoffoelsner.com, if you'd care to hear as well as see the larger patchwork pattern of my creative labors.)

The memoir begins with a few brief memories from my early childhood, moves on into my adolescence, when a lot more energy and awareness came to the fore in my life, and proceeds into accounts of events which proliferated in my twenties and thirties, continuing with stories from my midlife years.

I very much enjoy sharing my stories of the non-ordinary when people seem genuinely interested, and I've always been fascinated by others' accounts of their own mysterious experiences. However, enjoyment and fascination alone weren't compelling enough to motivate me to write this book. I recorded these personal reports in hope that they might strengthen readers' confidence in the breadth of our human potential.

This book also sprang from the same specific impetus as my sermon for the Unitarians: to affirm to readers that we can positively affect the environment through contemplative and creative expressions of benevolent intention and energy. I hope my anecdotes will move people to consider the implications of our innate "interbeing," a word coined by the Vietnamese Buddhist teacher Thich Nhat Hanh to denote the interconnectedness and interdependence of all that exists.

Here's another way of seeing it: the Gaia theory or principle is an ecological theory proposing that the biosphere and all physical components of the earth are closely integrated parts of a complex interacting system that maintains stable climatic and biogeochemical conditions of this planet. Originally put forward by James Lovelock, the Gaia theory views the earth as a single organism. One single organism. If we are all interconnected, "interbeing" aspects of this singularity Gaia, it follows that our caring for the natural world can have some degree of power to nurture it. My experiences lead me to believe that we have the potential to consciously work together with Nature.

Not all of these narratives are descriptive of communions with Nature. As they accumulated, I saw that many of them are simply accounts of small moments of extrasensory insight or remarkable synchronicity. Taken all together, however, they paint an expansive picture of a responsive universe, one in which we synergistically "interbe" with the natural world and each other.

Nor are these stories about deep mystical revelations. So-called ordinary, non-ordinary, and mystical experiences all exist on an unbroken continuum: all are expressions, modifications, and revelations of the Sacred. To my mind, spiritual epiphanies and awakenings are more fundamental than the non-ordinary events I've reported in this book, in the sense of being closer to the heart of Reality, and thus more radically transformative. However, they also are often more purely subjective in character than much of what I've chosen to describe here, so I haven't included many unless they feature externally verifiable aspects.

Countless people have written inspiringly about their spiritual experiences. I've included poems and prose passages which may suggest something of the fragrant scent of the mystical, but have chosen to focus more on paranormal experiences here, partly because I find that they carry a particular kind of power to open our minds to our infinite potential. I have observed that people with a skeptical mindset may be more open to the implications of parapsychological research than to mystical writings, especially those writings which come wrapped in the packaging of a religious dogma.

What I have written here is meant equally for everyone; spiritual finders, seekers, skeptics, and those who simply have no current interest in the spiritual dimension of life. However, the intensity of my specific wish to reach skeptics stems from the formative experience of growing up in a family and a wider social circle of secularized Jews and Christians who threw the beautiful, unconditioned baby of spirituality out with the historically murky, tradition-bound bathwater of conventional religiosity. As I experienced my initial youthful discoveries of the psychic realm and the divine milieu, I found this wholesale rejection of the Spirit and the powers of the Spirit to be increasingly hard to accept.

I had a lot of fun connecting the dots as I recorded and pondered these accounts. I am very aware that some readers will possess more in-depth, mature perspectives than I regarding the variety of psychic experiences shared in this memoir. Writing it has certainly deepened my own understanding of our human capacities for accurate intuition and expanded awareness. I am describing a personal learning process here, one that is perhaps more varied and broad in character than it is deep. Living this process has engendered much wonder in me, as does close study of any aspect of our world or lives. I hope these stories will enhance your own sense of wonder.

Writing this book has also heightened my interest in the constructive possibilities of what David Spangler and Dorothy Maclean (an original founder of the Findhorn Community in Morayshire, Scotland) call "attunement" with Nature and its subtle sentient energies. You'll come upon descriptions of some of my own attunements in these pages.

When she visited us and taught in Arkansas in 1980, Dorothy explained attunement as a simple process of going within to a relatively quiet, meditative space; getting in touch with a sense of what she calls "the living silence," or the Sacred; then briefly holding a clear intention to commune with whatever one wishes. This may be as all-inclusive as the Sacred itself, or as particularized as a being of any kind. Next, one lets go of one's intention, rather like one needs to drop a letter in the mailbox in order for the message in it to reach its destination. Finally, one rests in receptivity and notes whatever response may come by way of insights, impressions, images, words, the felt sense of a particular presence, energetic sensations, or physical effects like goose bumps.

The above process bears some similarity to the practice of Samyama described by the ancient Indian sage Patanjali in the third book of his Yoga Sutras. It also features some parallels to Eugene Gendlin's practice of Focusing. There are many different ways to attune, but they all involve receptivity. Dorothy has written about her experiences with attunement in the collectively authored book The Findhorn Garden, and in her own books To Hear the Angels Sing, Choices of Love, and Seeds of Inspiration.

You can find a transcript of "The Doorway Process," and another foundational exercise for attuning to the Divinity within, in Appendix One of Dorothy's autobiography, Memoirs of an Ordinary Mystic (2010). Dorothy has found it possible to attune to any being after making a conscious connection with the Source of all beings. She writes, "Since most of us think of God as the highest spiritual reality, it might sound strange to 'start at the top.' You could think of it instead as beginning at the beginning: whatever has been made by God can be met through God." I highly recommend this inspiring book about the not at all ordinary life of a blessed and beautiful soul. A voice recording of Dorothy leading

5

"The Doorway Process" is also available, through the Lorian Association. The first part of this recording provides a fine guided introduction to her way of attunement.

Freya Secrest of the Lorian Association taught and traveled with Dorothy for ten years. In a communication to me, she wrote:

> Her whole approach is about connecting to the God within first. From there the contact with the nature world flows. Her links are through beauty, wonder, awe, and love. This is the first part of The Doorway Process and it illustrates her approach to attunement: get oneself resonating with the energies of love, wonder and beauty, all core generative energies of life, and one is able to be in tune with the life force at the heart of everything in the universe.

Love and blessing open us. They allow us access to life force, and thus to all life forms. Have you read The Secret Life of Plants? It came out in 1973, and in it authors Peter Tompkins and Christopher Bird described interactions and experiments with plants conducted by Luther Burbank and George Washington Carver, and later, people like Cleve Backster and Marcel Vogel. In a number of these pioneering experiments, plants showered with love grew faster, larger, and hardier than those in control groups which received no love (or worse, were bombarded with feelings of hate or violence). I know a few of the many people who successfully replicated these experiments after reading The Secret Life of Plants.

Actually, before I saw the book , I was already among the converted due to the time I'd spent living at the Findhorn Community. There in 1965, a garden planted on sandy soil with organic additives of little more than cow manure, grass clippings, and seaweed tested out completely satisfactorily for all nutrients, including rare trace elements, though the Morayshire County Agricultural Advisor considered this impossible at that time.

While at Findhorn, I participated in making the first batch of compost there, based on a recipe of specific organic materials that Dorothy received in an attunement. During my stays at the community in 1969 and 1970, I witnessed the amazing size and quality of vegetables that grew in the ambient field of love and cooperation which we co-created with the devas and spirits of Nature.

Controlled scientific experiments in which human conscious-ness, and in some cases music, have demonstrably affected the structure and quality of plants, water, air, and soil have been con-ducted for decades. They continue to this day. I want to share a notable example of such research. The following may be an even greater stretch for some folks to take in than any of my little stories. Here goes:

In 2010, my partner Leslie and I traveled to Chicago to attend a weekend workshop with a man from India named Mahendra Kumar Trivedi. A mechanical engineer by training, he has an abil-ity to alter living and non-living matter with energy transmissions or "blessings" of focused intentional consciousness. Researchers in six countries from numerous scientific fields have gathered considerable data which substantiate his ability in a scientifically measurable manner. Here from the Trivedi Foundation website are outcomes of some of the Trivedi experiments:

- Without the use of chemical fertilizers or pesticides, crops showed significantly increased nutritional value.
- Crop yields increased up to 500%.
- Immunity in plants increased up to 639%.
- DNA (Genetics) altered up to 69% in plants and 79% in microbes.
- There were reduced concentrations of up to 99.81% in sam-ples of viruses that included HIV, Herpes and Hepatitis (both types B & C).
- Genus and species were altered in harmful bacteria.
- Human cancer cells were converted to non-cancerous cells. There are many testimonials from people Mr. Trivedi has apparently healed of a huge range of health problems.
- In material sciences research, the mass and size of atoms, and the energy within and between atoms changed significantly.
- In an experiment which Mr. Trivedi verbally reported to us in Chicago, the presence of radioactive isotopes was re-duced by up to 47% in contaminated water.
- The Trivedi Foundation also seeks to continue the research previously done on Mr. Trivedi's atypical physiology and its relationship to his unusual abilities.

This man's capacities have been tested in over four thousand laboratory and field experiments. Reports of experiments conducted with him have been published in peer-reviewed technical and medical journals, including the <u>Bulletin of Materials Science</u>, <u>Materials Research Innovations</u>, the <u>Metal Powder Report</u>, the on-line <u>Journal of Accord Integrative Medicine</u>, and <u>The Internet Journal of Alternative Medicine</u>.

While we were in Chicago, I experienced powerful and very relaxing energetic effects during the times set aside for group blessings. I found Mr. Trivedi an intriguing person: obviously focused and powerful, tempermental yet big-hearted, and somehow rather childlike. He spoke of the Divine in a tone of trust and truly reverent awe. If interested, you can google Ken Wilber's appreciative short essay on Mr. Trivedi and watch Deepak Chopra interview him on youtube. If still interested, you can visit the Trivedi Foundation website, and see a synopsized "Science Report" and many detailed laboratory reports.

The thing he said I liked the most was that he was participating in these experiments so that people will say, "This is also possible," in other words, to increase collective consensus that such abilities reside in us all to one degree or another. And that's why I've shared all this information with you, too.

If you do find the Trivedi experiments impossible, consider looking into what has been happening in the field of parapsychology over the last one hundred and fifty years. A fine place to start would be to read <u>Extraordinary Knowing: Science, Skepticism, and the Inexplicable Powers of the Human Mind</u> by Elizabeth Mayer, Ph.D., with a foreword by physicist Freeman Dyson, Institute for Advanced Study, Princeton, New Jersey.

The late Harold McCoy, a dowser and healer who founded the Ozark Research Institute in my home town, Fayetteville, Arkansas, played an essential role in the birth of Mayer's book. Her eleven year old daughter owned a rare and expensive harp which was stolen while the family was living in California. Harold, while in Fayetteville, successfully absent-dowsed over a map of Mayer's neighborhood in Oakland and located the exact street address of the house where her daughter's stolen harp was. Subsequently it was found and reclaimed, and that is what initially opened Mayer's previously skeptical mind to carrying out the research that led to her book. I was fortunate to have several opportunities to work jointly with Harold McCoy. You'll find another story about him, and how he found a precious lost object of mine, in the following pages.

Extrasensory, parapsychological, paranormal, supernatural, non-ordinary--look at those prefixes! They each imply a spirit/ matter split, a dualism that permeates some Eastern and most Western cultural and religious worldviews. Hopefully, someday this split will be culturally re-visioned, and the meaning of these words revised, so that we can accept all of our experiences--sensory, psychological, psychical, and spiritual--as normal, natural, ordinary aspects of our lives.

A cell phone might well appear supernatural to indigenous peoples in remote wilderness regions. Increased familiarity with phenomena of any kind allows us to accept it as natural. I hope this chronicle will encourage you to remember and consider your own unexplainable, perhaps unaccepted, experiences; the ones that so easily "fall through the cracks" in the concrete and are discounted and forgotten, since they run so utterly counter to our concretely consensual view of How Things Are.

This overview is over--now for some stories. As you read, may you feel further empowered to make a contribution to local and global environmental harmony through your focused love and intentions.

I. Childhood Experiences

("The Child is father of the Man"
--William Wordsworth, 1802)

At One with Mun (1950 and 1963)

Kansas City: One day in my fourteenth year, my maternal grandmother "Munnie" brings me home from a visit. She parks in the driveway, I get out of her car, and apropos of nothing that's been discussed, tell her that I know she has a tummy ache. She says that's true! We're both surprised. Not knowing how I know, I know. It's an early empathic insight.

There is an even earlier energetic bond with Munnie which I suddenly and dramatically recollect during a Tibetan Buddhist Dzogchen retreat led by Lama Surya Das in the late nineties. Meditating there, I viscerally remember lying in my baby buggy as she pushes it vigorously down the sidewalk past the evergreen bushes on the corner at 100 Morningside Drive. I'm loving it--the speed, the little bumps-ups at each gap between sections of concrete, and Munnie's zestful energy. In fact, in this crystal clear body memory, I *am* Munnie, just as much as I am Geoffie. I feel her body as distinctly as my own. There's nothing at all strange to me about this sense of oneness. It's utterly familiar and comfy-feeling. Perhaps it's what allows for my stomach ache intuition thirteen years later and one hundred feet away from the scene of our baby buggy communion.

Munnie's mother, Clara, whom I never met, descended from Scottish Canadians and brought that Scottish "second sight" with her. As a housewife in Hinckley, Minnesota, from time to time Clara would tell her household employees to set extra places at the table because a given number of guests were going to arrive unannounced, which they then would. So there's a psychic side to Munnie's life and bloodline.

I called my grandmother "Munnie" from toddlerhood, and perhaps from before that: the word "Mani" means "jewel" in Sanskrit. In fact, it is chanted daily by millions of Tibetan Buddhists, in the mantra OM MANI PADME HUM, which roughly translates, "Blessed be the jewel in the lotus." This is the mantra of Chenrezig, the Tibetan Buddhist deity of compassion. Tibetans consider His Holiness the Dalai Lama to be an incarnation or "emanation" of Chenrezig. Of course, it is quite possible that I was privy to some early, charged family discussion about "money" and later parroted the word in my grandmother's presence! In any event, it was construed and spelled as "Munnie" by the adults in my family.

First Religious Stirrings (1953)

Munnie takes me to the third floor of the Nelson Atkins Art Gallery in Kansas City, to a magnificent high-ceilinged Buddhist temple room. I'm four years old. Backed by faded but still wondrously colorful fresco paintings of lotus-lands and illumined arhats and bodhisattvas, a tall central seated figure of Kuan Yin is the visual and energetic center of the numinous room. In darker corners of the room dwell graceful statues of other, smaller Kuan Yins. He/she is venerated in different Asian cultures in both male and female forms; known by names like Avalokiteshvara, Chenrezig, Kuan Yin, Kannon, the Goddess of Mercy, and She Who Hears the Cries of the World.

My grandmother ushers me around the Gallery and into the hushed temple, allowing ample time for exploration. I lie face down on the cool tiled floor in a full prostration, directly below a willowy Kuan Yin, all pale and shimmering in the natural half-light of this huge stone room where every sound has its own partnering echo. After awhile I rise, and ask my grandmother, "Do you think the lady will be pleased with me?" My first religious impulses.

Years later, when beginning study and practice of the Buddhadharma, I'm introduced by my Tibetan teachers to Chenrezig's mantra, and I'm taught the way to do full body prostrations, exactly what I'd done that day in front of Kuan Yin's kindly Chinese form, there on the third floor of the echoey Nelson Gallery.

Old Sea Captain (1957)

I'm playing with the two Brower boys in their house across the street from my family's place on Morningside Drive. It's a quiet

Kansas City afternoon. I'm peering out wide living room windows which look down on the street and sidewalk. Coming up the sidewalk is a mystifying figure: it's an old man with a bushy white beard, wearing a sea captain's old-fashioned dark blue uniform and cap. He has a wooden peg leg girded by two metal bands, and he's heading past the Brower's house and up the hill. I call my two pals to the window and they see what I see. He makes it up the hill, around a curve and is gone. It's completely baffling.

I don't know if this qualifies as a story of a non-ordinary occurrence, really. The old gentleman looked three dimensional enough, stumping his way along, but it certainly remains in my memory as a dramatic example of the way life can deliver unexpected surprises right in the midst of the mundane.

Mooning Myself (1958)

I receive a telescope for my ninth birthday. One full moon night at Prairie Lee Lake, I train it up at the sky and catch the moon in its lens, a bright bubble wavering into focus. A shock shoots down the tube from moon to me: I seem to be looking at *myself* as I gaze into the moon's old bulbous pock-marked face. This early episode of sudden oneness startles me so much that I rarely use the telescope thereafter.

In the mid-nineteen nineties, I read passages from a biography of Dharma Lord Gampopa (1079-1153 CE), the foremost disciple of the highly realized Tibetan master Milarepa (1052-1135 CE), and remember my disconcerting little experience with the telescope, a walk in the park in comparison with Gampopa's extensions of consciousness. During one cave retreat, Gampopa felt all "three thousand world systems" in the universe spinning like a wheel, became dizzy and nauseated, and vomited repeatedly. Even very evolved people may have difficulty tolerating and integrating new, unexpected expansions of awareness.

My face-to-face union in space with the moon is a bit more of a bite than I can chew at that age.

Looking Back

As I review these early childhood experiences, I'm struck by how few memories I retain of anything out of the ordinary. This makes perfect sense, as my developmental task at that stage was to coalesce a Geoff, a definite identity in relationship with the other discrete beings in my family. I didn't bond well with my mother, but there were reassuring elements of closeness and even intimations of oneness in my relationship with my maternal grandmother. Her husband, Ernie, was my most beloved grandparent, and a very keen observer of Nature. Together we explored the worlds of birds and insects, and he helped me start my first rock collection. He taught me the basics of carpentry, and to ice skate and fish and row a boat. I began to compensate for the energetic and emotional distance from my mother by establishing a sustaining connection with Mother Nature herself, at the lake where Ernie built a cabin and later a boat, in the sanctuary of treehouses, and while happily bird watching. And my early affinity for Buddhist art signalled a natural gravitation to the Divine Feminine in the tender, motherly person of Kuan Yin.

From time to time, I was aware of a vague underlying sense of the immensity of space itself. In addition to my uneasy mergence with the moon, I can clearly remember blissfully crawling about in a warm golden ocean of sundust as light streamed into our home through a large eastern window. I must have been one or two years old when this happened. I also recall curling up in the darkness of a cozy little cupboard at around age six or seven, trying to wrap my mind around the notion that the sky goes on forever in all directions. Someone had told me that this is so, but I couldn't visualize it at first without picturing a sort of retaining wall around the far reaches of space. When I would go to mentally remove that wall, I felt an intriguing but slightly sickening sensation of spinning inside and around my body, which seemed to be suspended in an infinite expanse. I've compared notes with a lot of people who recollect engaging in this kind of space exploration, and becoming thoroughly mind-boggled while pondering infinity, at around the same age.

In sum, there was an occasional relaxation of the boundaries between my developing sense of being a circumscribed self, and Something vast and elusive. At times that Something seemed rather impersonal, skylike, and unsettling to experience; at other times more personal, earthy, and humanly hospitable. Once in a while, a memorable moment of simultaneity surfaced in my awareness, in which I experienced both the vast and the circumscribed at once. All these brief episodes of variously dissociated and more embodied awareness grew to be more frequent and compelling as I approached adolescence.

II. Adolescence:
Awakening Energy and Awareness

"I'm in Another Body!" (1962-1966 and later)

When I'm thirteen my mother introduces me to the work of J. D. Salinger: <u>Catcher in the Rye</u> and <u>Nine Stories</u>. The humor in Catcher is lost on me--it's serious; the ruminations of an older teen. But the last story in <u>Nine Stories</u> is of great magnetic interest. The nondual Vedantists of Hinduism and the doctrine of reincarnation are mentioned there. I'm most grateful to my mother for bringing Salinger to my attention. Shortly thereafter she shows me a newspaper article about the Ramakrishna Vedanta Society of Kansas City, and I begin to attend their meetings. Considering Mom's complete lack of attraction to anything religious, I'm especially touched by her support and sensitivity to my emerging interests.

Past life proclivities? Possibly. Anyway, an inchoate yearning for spiritual experience arises after I read "Teddy," that ninth Salinger story. I sit on my bedroom floor and try to meditate, then get in bed and am startled when I fall into a cataleptic state, body buzzing with energy; energy locked in moveless limbs. I'm frightened yet deeply intrigued by this sudden surge which can't be easily accommodated or assimilated. Not yet.

Years pass. We move to a new house. I occupy a corner room with a nice view of old elm and maple trees. Over those growing years I find my way to more fulfilling friendships and self-expressions (music-making, poetry, a Unitarian youth group). I continue to be ambushed at the edge of sleep by this odd and unnerving cataleptic state from time to time.

At age fifteen, I meet the landscape artist Robert Sudlow, my wise and supportive friend from that time on. Bob introduces me to J.R.R.Tolkien, to Odilon Redon and Morris Graves' artwork, to Ralph Vaughn Williams' music, and so many other wonderful artistic depth-markers of the heart. He also acquaints me with Bach's "St. Matthew Passion (1727)."

Robert Sudlow

I have an old turntable across from my bed, a vital focus in so many teenage bedrooms, "my music" being absolutely key at that age. I discover that lying down and listening to the five-record set of the giant orchestral-choral layer cake of Bach's ecstatic "Passion" can predictably elicit the compelling yet unsettling energetic rush I experienced at age thirteen after my first attempted meditation.

At seventeen, the game changes for me. I meet a soulful, peaches-and-creamy girl at the All Souls Unitarian Church. From 0 on the "sexometer," I accelerate up the sexuality scale to 60. This sweet, sensitive girl inaugurates a new era of unexpected sensual tenderness in my life.

Along with this new sexual dispensation comes electric sensation. I lie in bed and stream with energy. The cataleptic episodes come more often, with torrential force. Energies ascend my spine like mercury zooming up a thermometer on a summer day. I'm completely ignorant of writings about kundalini, auras, and the like, though not completely in the dark about trance states, due to reading an early biography of Edgar Cayce, entitled <u>There Is a River</u> .

Each day after school for four days, I cloister myself in my room, determined to move through the now-familiar, paralyzing fear and to break through to whatever state beckons from beyond it. I drop the blinds, and listen to "St. Matthew Passion" while supine. For the first three of these days, I ride the rapturous voices into that charged hypnagogic state of half-sleep-and-half-awakeness where my energy surges, but won't fully release and flow. I end up in catalepsy, sensing a great potential for as yet undiscovered depths. How to proceed?

On the fourth afternoon, toward early evening, I listen for awhile, plunge into that electrified medium yet again, but this time to my startled delight, I rise from the bed, feeling amazingly weightless, and walk toward the door, all a-sparkle with energy. Upon reaching the door, I simply walk right through it. I stand by the stairway in wonder, feeling my body, ignited at all its infinitesimal points, and realize (logic prevails here) that I've just walked through a solid door and that therefore "I'm in another body!" This recognition jolts me back into my bedroom, where I instantly re-enter my resting form.

I come back most enlivened, having at last passed beyond the cataleptic barrier, the previously impassable portal to greater depth and new freedom of movement in a subtle, imaginal dimension. So begins a period of what one might call training: I learn to navigate in a plane of energetic counterparts to physical reality, through fluid, changing landscapes; some identical to the street and tree scenes around our home, some very foreign to me. I visit green meadows where flowers bloom in colors never seen by physical eyes. There are sudden flights into cloudy, tumbling skyscapes, or plummets into deep sea waters. These experiences are alternately and sometimes simultaneously terrifying and ecstatic.

Here's an early poem about this miraculous new sense of access to space and landscape:

First Ways Of Flight

I found a wakened way
to fly my slightest dream
across the prairie, wireless,
tree to tree. At times barbed wire
and taut black talk-lines
sliced my flight. They stung
and nettled my dream-body,
just as they overhung and netted
this country. Encroaching suburbs
sometimes held me from
full span. Clenched fists
of smoke from factories;
dense inner cities pulled
on me. Yet I was willingly
drawn down to certain altars,
shrines, archways, parks,
side roads, homes, and human
gatherings where primal silence
reasserts itself. Then I could begin
to glide once more on amber
waves of light East-West
above the land. My being
sought sanctuary in mountains
and rivers, at estuaries of Spirit.
I rested in slow-breathing meadows
far from men. Night after night,
these dreams moved me in vision-flight
beyond a life I had thought mine,
on through the gray where worlds meet,
into a country where all colors
are sacred and alive.

In addition to such excursions into Nature, there are lucid dream-meetings. An especially vivid one features a teenage girl from a small town in Indiana who tells me she too travels on what I learn occultists and Theosophists have called "the astral plane." There are also dismaying yet humorous lessons in getting used to this new, permeable milieu: I repeatedly get stuck, all gluey, in our home's attic ceiling, and must remind myself I'm in another, less densified body. Then, once having registered that, I pass quickly through the roof into the upper air, no longer stalled.

I'm tutored by these astral-plane or lucid dream experiences for years, sometimes appearing in other's dreams, or even materializing (unbeknownst to me) in the room of a completely astounded young Unitarian pal from Nebraska, or 'visiting' my grandmother one night, only to hear from her a few days later, "Did you...uh... come see me?"

Curious, I explore other peoples' reports of their out-of-body experiences (OBE's). The Projection of the Astral Body by Carrington and Muldoon is a helpful resource. Chapter 43 of The Autobiography of a Yogi by Paramahansa Yogananda offers many insights. (Incidentally, Yogananda dedicated this book to Luther Burbank, the pioneering American botanist and horticulturist, who employed a highly refined intuition in his work with plants). A little later on, I find parallels between my own experiences and those of Robert Monroe, whose first of several books on his OBE's, Journeys Out of the Body, is a classic in the literature on this fascinating phenomenon.

In 1970, I meet Michael Murphy while attending a spiritual gathering in Britain with some friends from the Findhorn Community. Co-founder of the Esalen Institute and a key player in the early development of the Human Potential Movement, in the years since 1970 Murphy has chronicled accounts of OBE's and a huge range of other extraordinary human abilities in novels like Jacob Atabet, Golf in the Kingdom (also a feature film) and in nonfiction books like The Psychic Side of Sports. His masterwork is The Future of the Body, of which philosopher Stephen Phillips has written, "Not since William James' The Varieties of Religious Experience has there appeared such a galvanizing probe into uncommon human capacities."

In Hinduism and Buddhism, these capacties are known as "siddhis." "Siddhi" is a Sanskrit noun that can be translated as"perfection," "attainment," "success," or "accomplishment." One can find a full discussion of these siddhis and how to evoke them in Patanjali's Yoga Sutras (dated by different Indologists as written somewhere between 200 BCE and 500 CE). They may appear spontaneously, or be transmitted from one person to another under certain conditions of receptivity and readiness; or they can be generated either intentionally or unintentionally through the use of certain herbs, rituals and mantras, through deep meditation, or by various specialized forms of self-discipline.

Mystics from all of the world's religious traditions generally view siddhis as distractions from the goal of spiritual realization. Exceptions to this perspective can be found, including in the written teachings of Michael Murphy's teacher Sri Aurobindo Ghose (1872-1950), who considered the presence and benevolent use of siddhis to be a functional attribute of many great saints, and quite often of geniuses. Aurobindo intuited that we are in a time of accelerating transformation and that psychic development can be a legitimate facet of that quickening. Like his teacher, Murphy sees the siddhis as potentially wholesome expressions of individual spiritual maturation and indicators of our collective evolutionary aptitude.

Maharishi Mahesh Yogi (1917 or 1918-2008) developed a program for eliciting siddhis via a combination of Transcendental Meditation and Patanjali's practices, with the rationale that cultivating them in a balanced way can contribute to the purification of the human nervous system, and thus accelerate a meditator's spiritual development and bring increased "coherence" and peace to her immediate environment and the world. Thousands of meditators gather to practice Maharishi's TM-Sidhi program with those shared intentions. Maharishi's TM-Sidhi program contributed to my own unfoldment, and I am inclined to agree with his take on this, but cautiously and with qualifications, depending upon the unique developmental tasks and capacities of each person.

Neither Aurobindo nor Maharishi Mahesh Yogi saw the siddhis as necessarily posing impediments to spiritual realization. Ripeness is all. Support from others with wisdom and experience can be crucial. Under favorable conditions, they may be harbingers or by-products of greater spiritual awareness. They may open us

20

up. On the other hand, they may be destabilizing sidetracks, corruptive, or worse. My own limited but vivid experience of siddhis has made me hungrier; not for more power, but for a deeper surrender to the all-inclusive power of Reality.

As my OBE's and other psychic experiences amplify my sense of what we are and can yet be, I begin to delve into an essential question: "What does this imply about our True Nature?" It's clear to me that the scintillating rainbow snow of the astral plane has an even more primal Source in formlessness.

I receive hints of a path back to that Source. For instance, during one brief projection as a sphere of pellucid pure awareness with a 360' degree field of vision, I hover for a moment near that portal-opening record player before yet again rejoining my buzzing energetic hive-like seventeen year old body. Descending, spinning down, lowering back into my physical form, I open astonished eyes which for some time thereafter seem less confined to the dense, literal scenes I see as I look out upon the external world. I begin to sense how all experiences, physical and more subtle, arise and are held in a field of pure potential, pure awareness, pure Mystery. This process illustrates one way that the emergence of siddhis or paranormal experiences can help orient us to a more holistic, inclusive recognition of What Is.

As the seasons turn, an associated and perhaps more fully integrated phenomenon occurs increasingly often: rather than separating from physical awareness, I remain well-grounded in my body while simultaneously experiencing myself at, and sometimes *as*, another location. Sometimes I walk about such locations after "remote viewing " them, and actually discover things there which I've previously seen in visionary visitations. Later in these pages, I share accounts of such viewings, and of wondrous mergings with mineral, plant, and human features of particular landscapes. Many hundreds of these experiences have enhanced my felt sense of oneness with the environment, and, more fundamentally, with all life. Here is a poetic account of one such subtle bilocation:

Earth's Door Opens

The prelude
to this reverie's a walk

21

I take in winter woods
after a cold hard rain,
exploring hills and hollows
in the sloping zone
between the nearby countryside
and my suburban home.

That night, I move through
those same woods again
as I rest awake in bed.
If I have a form there,
it's composed of earth and air
more than something human.
I'm both
observer and observed.
I feel the contours
and the complex textures
of the living land,
and see moist, muddy earth
up close.
The scene is "lovely,
dark, and deep,"
as Robert Frost wrote;
refreshing and sustaining
to my spirit.

Something sustaining and enlightening asserts itself in all of these experiences. They seem to signal an evolving fluidity of identity and awareness. They present a door through which I glimpse a little more of what we truly are.

Such experiences also begin to bring forward a sense of some kind of effortless, benign exchange happening between myself and the natural world, an intuition which is later reinforced at Findhorn Community and elsewhere. In his little gem of a book

<u>Stillness Speaks</u>, author Eckhart Tolle writes wonderfully about this 'sacred exchange':

> You need nature as your teacher to help you reconnect with Being. But not only do you need nature, it also needs you.

> You are not separate from nature. We are all part of the One Life that manifests itself in countless forms throughout the universe, forms that are all completely interconnected. When you recognize the sacredness, the beauty, the incredible stillness and dignity in which a flower or a tree exists, you add something to the flower or the tree. Through your recognition, your awareness, nature too comes to know itself. It comes to know its own beauty and sacredness through you!

> ...Nature can bring you to stillness, That is its gift to you. When you perceive and join with nature in the field of stillness, that field becomes permeated with your awareness. That is your gift to nature.

How'd She Know I Knew? (1963)

I'm about fourteen in this one. I'm sitting at the kitchen table as my father enters the room. My mother's already there. She tells me and my dad that she's thinking of a specific number between 1 and 10, and asks me to guess the number. "Seven," I say, and that turns out to be right. It's not all that impressive, since the odds are 1 in 10, but Mom says, "See, I told you," to my dad.

What prompted this demonstration for Dad? Had I unknowingly spoken thoughts that were going through Mom's mind at some juncture? Did this kind of sensitivity perhaps unnerve her? That's the only mention of ESP I can recall from either of my parents in my entire childhood, except once when my mother tells me that a person she respects believes in telepathy. She never brings the topic up for discussion again.

Monkey Say (1965)

Kansas City: My friend Maple and I are playing blues harmonica together in an early hippie apartment. The older (early twenties!) proto-hippie lady of the place, is serenely stitching away at a needlepoint design that reads, " God Bless Our Pad." All this seems ineffably cool to me.

Our interweaving harmonica playing crescendos over and over, and as we get more and more synced in with each other, some kind of mind-meld occurs and we suddenly stop simultaneously, lower our Hohner Marine band blue harps from our lips, gaze meaningfully at each other as if we are each about to share the Secret of the Ages known only to our sixteen year old selves, and loudly exclaim "Monkey!" at the same time. Early drug-free hippie telepathy.

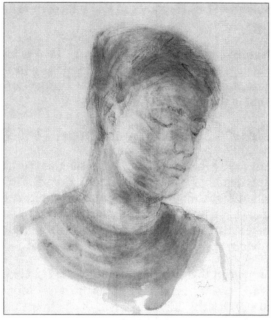

Drawing of Geoffrey Oelsner
by Robert Sudlow (1967)

Now You See It (1966)

I meet Dr. Hawk. He tells me how he hypnotized himself and changed the color of his eyes overnight. They're a startling blue.

He has enormous presence, this whip-thin Florida chiropractor out on the road with his quiet, cute Southern paramour, floating around the country in a big white Cadillac, all full of powers and mojo. We sit in a mutual friend's pad in Kansas City. As Clyde Hawk holds forth from the sofa, cigarette vaguely wand-like in his gesticulating hand, I begin to see a yellow vapor around him. I ask what it is and am told " That's my aura," and from that night on I've often seen them, sometimes surrounding people as colored envelopes or clear bubbles or undulant like heat-waves; some-times as blue, green, and yellow clouds or fluxes of energy in my night-darkened room. Dr. Hawk stirs some stuff awake in me.

So much energy moves through me for days after this initial opening that at one point while taking inventory in the warehouse where I have a summer job, I look at a nearby metal stool, expe-rience a huge bulge of power at my hara (a Japanese term for a subtle center in the nerve plexus of the lower abdomen), then turn away and hear the stool crash down to the floor behind me. No one else is around. No physical contact is involved. Forceful, fer-vid energy begins to flow that hot, discovery summer.

"It's 452!" (1967)

It's lunch time at the boy's school I attend from grades two to twelve. I've been sitting at a science teacher's table in the cafeteria--his name is Mr. Vibert. An announcement is made at the end of lunch: Tomorrow there'll be a big prize drawing for... for what I don't remember. Anyway, we're shown a large glass jar filled with beans, and told to guess the exact number of beans in it. Who-ever's guess is closest wins. I say to the whole table, clearly and confidently, "It's 452! Remember I said that tomorrow: 452." The whole improbable claim just comes rushing out with no premeditation.

Fast forward to the next day; same place. We sit at Mr. Vibert's table prepared for the number to be drawn. I remind the guys, "Remember, I said it's 452." And it is! Mr. Vibert's mind is sud-denly forced to open to the possibility of precognition. Though a scientific thinker, he's unlike some who would unscientifically discount such impressive evidence. In fact, a year later during my freshman year at college, I get a letter from a younger friend from the same school who's had a strange, lucid dream experience which features a non-human entity. He wants to understand this bewildering dream, and since Mr. Vibert serves as his academic advisor and is someone he trusts, my friend relates the dream to him, and Tom Vibert suggests he write me, describing the dream and asking for insight into it. It's interesting how we get from 452 to dream interpretation here.

In fact, I do have some insights to offer about the possible nature of the oddly solid dreamscape where my friend has encountered an apparently non-human energy. So that lottery leads to two helpful openings.

The Lovers (1968 and later)

Oberlin, Ohio: I'm sitting at the Campus Restaurant with my friend the poet Sandford Lyne (later, the author of In the Footsteps of Paradise, Writing Poetry from the Inside Out, and other wonderful books). I show him my Tarot cards, acquired a few years earlier in Greenwich Village when a black-Puerto Rican gentleman named Joe advised my purchase of this deck, the so-called Rider Deck designed by occultist Arthur Edward Waite and clairvoyant artist Pamela Coleman Smith. My friend Cam and I accompanied Joe back to his Harlem apartment where he showed us how to read the cards, transmitting an attitude and an intensity to me that contributed to my confidence in the synchronicity and rightness of the card readings I subsequently did.

Now I sit across from Sandy Lyne at a booth, and begin a reading for him. He's a senior, I'm a freshman at Oberlin College. He's been extremely kind to me, interested and outgoing. I want to give him a good demonstration of the Tarot, so I summon up something like the intense focus I saw Joe generate when he read for us in the cramped Harlem apartment where so much went down in the summer of 1966.

Soon I find a kind of energetic groove, and everything disappears except the deck of Tarot cards and my sense of Sandy's observant presence. I draw a single card out from the deck without turning it up, and slap it face down on the table. "The Lovers!" Those words leap out of my mouth, then I turn the sole card over. It is indeed, "The Lovers," a man and woman basking in the brightness of a radiant angel stationed between them, a towering cosmic figure of solar fire.

There are seventy-eight cards in the Tarot deck, so my chance of calling the card correctly stand at one in seventy-eight. Sandy's mouth falls open in astonishment. I'm surprised myself, and gratified to have been able to clearly manifest the magic of the Tarot, and to demonstrate either synchronicity or outright precognition for my friend.

The most exceptional Tarot reader I have had the good fortune to meet was also a spiritualistic trance medium and seer from British Columbia named William F. Balderstone. After graduating from high school in 1967, I bought a ninety-nine dollar bus ticket that allowed me to travel out to the West Coast, north to Canada, then back home again to Kansas City. I met Mr. Balderstone in a little metaphysical bookstore in Vancouver, where he gave me a life-changing life-reading with Tarot cards from the Rider Deck.

People who are expert at divination tend to be naturally intuitive, but even more powerfully so when they focus their intuition through the "lens" of a divinatory system that they find evocative. It was evident to me that Mr. Balderstone received a steady influx of psychic insights while contemplating the images of the cards that he turned up. Clearly, he shared much more than a simple by-the-book interpretation of those rich images.

Almost all of what he sensed and predicted about me has come true, including certain difficulties which happened in my twenty-third year just as he foretold. His understanding of the kinds of work I'm best suited for has also proven to be remarkably nuanced and accurate. Every few years, I listen to the old cassette tape I made of the even older reel-to-reel audiotape Mr. Balderstone used to record his reading with me, and I still find it relevant. At one moment in the reading, he said something to me that caused my consciousness to expand dramatically. Without my saying a word about what had just transpired, Mr. Balderstone immediately picked up on it, exclaiming, "Now that we have you in a state of grace, how are we going to help keep you there?" That's a precious memory from a brief but important meeting with someone who died long ago. Love wells up in my heart as I recall the old seer.

Over the following years, I receive Tarot and other kinds of divinatory readings of considerable descriptive and predictive accuracy from time to time. These include my partner Leslie's unerringly helpful readings from the Motherpeace Tarot deck;

numerological and astrological readings replete with specific, spot-on information and insights; and, most amazingly, consultations with an intuitive named Beverly Bright, who uses many approaches to bring through helpful material.

Beverly has done a number of consultations with Leslie and me based on the complex and revealing Human Design system. Her ability to tune in and to communicate what she sees is nothing short of astounding. At one point, I asked her for a reading on a friend of mine who was facing some life-challenges. She had never met or had any appreciable knowledge of this person. I feverishly transcribed nine single-spaced pages in longhand as she shared her interpretation of my friend's Human Design chart, and afterwards was unable to find a single item that failed to ring true or fell short of providing a valuable fresh perspective. The reading offered a perceptive overview, and touched on scores of pertinent details of my friend's life.

This kind of experience has provided me with further confirmation of the efficacy of focused intuition. As a psychotherapist, I've always felt motivated to hone my own intuition about the people I work with. Getting a feel for the different ways such gifted readers work has supplied me with hints about how to cultivate my own intuitive abilities.

Looking Back

Newness! With adolescence came new aliveness: poetry and song-making; creative new friends; the advent of first love, and with it awakening sexuality and energetic activation; a newfound fluidity of consciousness marked by experiences of lucid dreaming and out-of-body journeying; and incidents of clairvoyance and visionary experience. As I began to see auric fields flux around people, I was startled by the insight that we can view our worlds in very divergent ways, depending upon the particular quality of our consciousness at a given time.

Backpacking trips at a wonderful summer camp for boys in the Rocky Mountains of Colorado opened me to communion with the natural world. I sensed the living silence that rings from ridge to ridge, grew physically stronger, and returned to urban life changed, suddenly uninterested in television and in some essential way turned expectantly toward the center of my own being. Psychic and mystical experience co-emerged in me with the arising of a fresh sensitivity to Nature.

In the midst of this formative period, the artist Robert Sudlow became my friend. For him, the act of painting landscapes was an offering of love and praise. I distinctly felt the circular character of this offering; how Bob's seeing and receiving of a scene looped back outward as he painted and joyfully radiated positive energy forth into the place he was depicting. Sudlow made me aware of the possibility of developing a sacramental relationship with Nature. Witnessing his creative process over and over again worked a gentle transformative magic in me. I spent more time outdoors, lingering under trees, playing my guitar and singing songs to the wind. Mine was in many ways a very typical adolescence, awkward and often tumultuous, and concurrently a blessed time of connection and discovery.

III. Young Adulthood

("Your young men will see visions" --Joel 2:28)

"Coo Coo Coo" (1969)

I'm at a UFO convention in northwestern Pennsylvania with Maryona, my spiritual teacher at that time, and some pretty strange folks. I've pitched my pup tent on a small rise in a little rolling field bordered by forest. During the first night I'm there, it starts to rain. I'm lying in my sleeping bag half-awake, when I'm startled by the loud sound of a human voice imitating a bird-call: "Coo, coo, coo!" This voice resounds from my solar plexus, but I experience it as originating from an entity that's native to the area, and that definitely wants me to vacate that exact spot.

Along with the bird calls come a barrage of verbal and energetic cues that clearly communicate, "Get out! Get up and get out of here now!" I'm spooked, but bravely reply back mentally, "I'm sorry, but it's raining, it's night, and I'm not moving." I fall back asleep after this, and the rest of the night passes uneventfully.

The next morning, as I sit outside my tent in front of a friendly little campfire, another participant at the convention saunters into the clearing, and with a slight smile on his face asks me how I've slept. When I describe to him what happened in the night, he says, "You're camping on an Indian burial mound."

This gentleman's a Susquehannock Indian from southern Pennsylvania, from a tribal group of extraordinarily tall, physically powerful people, which was allied with the Iroquois Confederacy. He explains to me that as youth, the people once native to this place each selected a personal spot to go to for prayer, and throughout their lives took a scoop of dirt there each time they went to pray and commune with the Great Spirit. Gradually, each prayer-spot grew into a mound, and at the time of death, these people were then customarily buried in their own prayer-mounds.

My new friend, Chief Lightfoot Talking Eagle (Tom Appleton) tells me that I've slept on top of one of these ancient burial places, and have disturbed either the spirit of the deceased, or a guardian spirit still keeping vigil there. He shows me how to build a campfire upon arriving at a new place, and to send up prayers and loving intentions on the ascending woodsmoke for harmonious relations with all beings in the vicinity. I've done that ever since when setting up camp.

Chief Lightfoot Talking Eagle's life as he described it to me was full of miraculous happenings and interfaces with the Spirit World, starting powerfully at age seven during a three day visionary period shut in total darkness in a special earthen hut. The aptitude he showed for spiritual journeying (out-of-body travel) and revelation led his elders to select him from three young male candidates for early training as a tribal medicine person. In addition to earning a master's degree at Yale, he gave himself to a lifelong course of learning in what he called "the forty-four houses of the University of the Universe."

Lightfoot Talking Eagle and his wife Fleet Deer befriend me during the unconventional convention where we meet, walking with me in the woods and sharing observations of the visible and invisible ecology of the area. He confidently tells me that the spirits of the woodlands love to hang around me, because I go out in the woods alone to sing and play, which is true, though I haven't mentioned that to him. I still think of him and Fleet Deer often, though they passed beyond the mortal veil some decades ago.

After connecting with Lightfoot Talking Eagle, I begin to intuit what seems to be the long-lingering presence of various Native American peoples as I travel about the country. The following poem expresses such an intuitive inkling, which comes to me at a rest stop in southern Colorado:

On Them

"The Ute were a very dirty people,"
says the white mountain-biker to his two friends
at a rest-stop by the Colorado River.
I think to myself, "You're standing on them, sir."

31

We're all standing on them, as we walk this continent where indigenous peoples have lived in great harmony with their environments for untold thousands of years. Can we be aware of this fact and let that awareness inspire us to greater reverence and deference for them, and for the land we also now belong to?

Journeying Out of the Body with Judy (1969)

On the Sky's Beach in Virginia

A woman bore eight children
in that cabin on the ledge,
and when I came to stay a night
with friends who'd bought the place
I heard them
running in and out
the screen door,
in the yard.
That family hated leaving there.

But their father met his match
in moonshine from a nearby
shady grove.
Above his head
the Virginia sky reeled
and thin-boned trees
swayed on the upper ridge
like dreams of unborn children.
They lived there twenty-three years.

High cliffs of rain
ached down on us all night.
In early morning,
clouds glyphed out over the plain,
leaving the moon
to disturb our sleep.
Swimming the floor,
it shifted through our dreaming hair.

I stirred her, my friend
next to me in a down cocoon,
and we inched out of our bodies;
slipped *through* the backdoor
and up the ridge in moonlight.
We sat on the sky's beach,
stars next to our faces.
Her body was white driftwood on that shore.
Then a sixth sense warned me
to leave her there
to receive what only she
was ready for.

Later, she returned
through the backdoor,
and lay beside me, whispering,
"Hold me.
The rocks are on fire.
Everything's speaking."

Judy still remembers this high energy out-of-body event we
consciously experienced together.

The Findhorn Community, Nature Spirits, and Crossing Paths with Chogyam Trungpa (1969–70)

Dorothy Maclean

For me, as for people in many if not all indigenous cultures, the spirits of Nature are expressions of the nature of Spirit just as we humans are, dynamic energies which are part of a larger holistic ecology. What I see and feel at the Findhorn Community opens my young mind to the possibilities of actually working with such energies in beneficial ways.

At this time in my life, I'm rather shy and often lonely. Peter and Eileen Caddy and Dorothy Maclean , the three co-founders of the community, are extremely kind to me during my stays there. At one point, Peter spends the better part of a day taking me to a number of powerful places in the area. One of them, Randolph's Leap, is said to be especially charged with the presence and energy of elves, fairies, and other subtle beings of Nature. I wonder now whether Peter received guidance to take me there in order to help prepare me for later, closer associations with such beings in the United States.

I cherish my memories of the Caddys' warmth, and of a particular day when Dorothy invites me to take afternoon tea with her in her snug little trailer home. An exquisite feeling of peace steals over me as I sit there in her sage and caring company. The center between and above my eyebrows "wakes" and pulsates with influxes of bright, vibratory energy.

A significant synchronicity happens to me at Findhorn early in 1970, when what will be two of the major threads in my spiritual life crisscross. While working at the community during a break from my studies at the University of Aberdeen, I see a small crowd of people gathered around a stocky Asian gentleman and a lovely young woman. Inquiring, I learn that the man is Chogyam Trungpa Rinpoche (1939-1987), and that he is one of two presiding lamas at a Tibetan monastery. Situated south of Findhorn in a peaceful valley on the banks of the river Esk in Scotland, Kagyu Samye Ling was the first Tibetan Buddhist Centre to have been established in the West. It is to this day a center for meditation in the Karma Kagyu tradition of Tibetan Buddhism.

Trungpa Rinpoche has just eloped with the sixteen year old Diana Pybus, and has come to Findhorn in search of some sanctuary and privacy from rapacious reporters, who are eagerly trying to squeeze as much sensationalism from the event as possible. As I follow him around with the rest of an impromptu little entourage, he pauses to play a silver hand drum. Trungpa radiates silence and power, and when I recall his presence I'm left with an indelible memory of something golden permeating him, and all of us there with him. In his beautiful book <u>Warrior-King of Shambala: Remembering Chogyam Trungpa</u>, Jeremy Hayward recounts similar impressions of a pervasive, golden quality noted by many of Chogyam Trungpa's students. Later, I write a poem to honor this charismatic, pioneering Buddhist teacher:

Bodhisattva

For Chogyam Trungpa Rinpoche

Your being fits behind
the sensitive masks
the world wears.

So you are love--
the wellspring that an open heart makes--
and you wear the heavens like a cowl.

So you are sheer
transparency;
pure water
that enters through dry mouths
the parched hearts of each
fellow creature.

I also wish to dedicate the above poem to another master of the Karma Kagyu order of Buddhism, His Holiness the 17th Karmapa, Ogyen Trinley Dorje. He is known as the oldest continuously, consciously reincarnating being in Tibetan Buddhism, and is a very great spiritual blessing to our planet. Born in Tibet in 1985, he currently lives in India. In 2008, Leslie and I travelled to his monastic seat in Woodstock, New York, to be among those to greet and receive teachings from H. H. the Karmapa on his first visit to America. Rainbow displays attended him there. His spiritual transmission was very palpable. The previous 16th Karmapa was one of Chogyam Trungpa's foremost teachers.

Trungpa Rinpoche's appearance at Findhorn makes sense. He felt a kinship with the community and its founders. Peter Caddy had some time earlier taken him to a spiritual healer in England after the car he was driving crashed into a "joke shop, " which injured him quite seriously. Trungpa later was to receive revelatory "Shambala teachings" which bear certain similarities to the Findhorn Community's cosmology, with its Nature spirits and angelic beings. The Shambala teaching lineage established by Trungpa includes texts and practices relating to "dralas," or sentient patterns of energy which have the capacity to enhance human and environmental well-being. The "drala principle" is an inherent aspect of most traditional cultures, involving beings variously envisioned as angels, devas, Nature spirits, elemental energies, and gods and goddesses.

Later I study with Trungpa at the first summer session of the Naropa Institute in Boulder, Colorado in 1974, and witness his body flash through extraordinary transformations as he manifests archetypal tantric energies. This begins my connection with Vajrayana Buddhism, particularly that of the Kagyu tradition, a spiritual strand which continues to run unbroken through my life to this day, along with my ongoing connection to the Findhorn Community and its influential present-day legacy.

The Heart of Scotland (1970)

The west coast of Scotland, near Oban: Twenty-one years old and lonesome in early spring, I wander the darkening pebble beach with a double shot of straight whiskey in me. Sad, drifting, I weave around over wet shadowy rocks. With a mind of its own, my right hand goes down for a barely-seen round rock. What I grab is surprisingly heavy for its size, and it instantly feels like mine. Later, in my room, I see its rounded redness, its seams of darker rust-red veins, the little spout holes on its domed surface, the smooth, finger-friendly indentations, and I know it to be a sort of simulacrum of a human heart--my own heart-stone. I have (or host) it still, and have carried it with me on many travels, including back to Scotland once to touch its native soil and soulful ocean homeland yet again.

The "Heart of Scotland," as I call my mineral friend, (not "my precious," mind you!) has been blessed by lamas and other holy folk. Most memorable is the blessing of a great Tibetan lama, a guest-teacher at a Dzogchen meditation retreat in upper New York State in 2000. I yearn to receive his blessing on the stone, and have it at the ready when we happen upon each other on our respective early morning walks. He holds it, concentrates his formidable attention on it and on the act of blessing, then blows mantras on and, as I soon discover, into it.

We part and I walk the heart-stone back to my room. There I set it down and sit myself, and very soon begin to circle from my body to the stone and back in consciousness, as if riding on some subtle current of breath. Over and over I pass through the little spout-holes into the heart of the heart-stone, then back out into my body. Over and over I am the stone as well as and as much as my own form. I marvel at the power of the lama's blessing.

37

Years later, in 1998, the Tibetan master Chetsang Rinpoche also holds and blesses the stone in Escondido, California. On being shown it, he immediately says, "It's a heart." And so it is to me, as well as being a repository of ocean sounds (wave-wash contouring it for millennia), and perhaps the benedictions of...who knows? ...earlier Druidic keepers who also recognized its beauty and sacred qualities, and most certainly of the kind lamas and other spiritual friends who've held and imbued it with their generous blessings.

First Healing Whodunit (1970)

Oberlin, Ohio: I've been working with Helen Spitler, aka Maryona, a Western spiritual teacher, during my student years at Oberlin College. She's led me through guided visualizations of inner light. Interestingly, the three colors I've seen for several years brightly swimming the darkness of my bedroom at night--blue, green, and golden yellow--are the three colors she introduces to me in visualizations as successive streams of cleansing (blue), healing (green), and spiritual blessing (gold).

On one occasion, as Maryona works with me, a great stream of energy seems to beam down into me and lift me high above the planet into a realm of light and wondrous lightness where I abide in some subtle way for days thereafter. This happens instantly after I make a prayer to be of benefit to all beings. On another occasion, Maryona tells me that I've received circular amethyst-colored centers in each palm which will facilitate the healing of others. I'm subsequently slow to share this supposed healing gift, not really knowing how to present it to fellow students, or to my immediate family members, a generally skeptical lot.

But now a young woman in an Oberlin dining hall tells me over dinner that she's had a skin rash on her foot that just won't go away despite her applying ointments of different kinds. I suggest a laying-on-of-hands, and she agrees. The next day, she excitedly reports that the rash has disappeared, and apparently it doesn't return. She's healed.

Years later, in my practice as a clinical social worker, I receive excellent training from faculty members of the American Society for Clinical Hypnosis, among them Dabney Ewen, M. D. of Tulane Medical School in New Orleans, who teaches us that skin conditions like viral warts and bacterial rashes are often susceptible to healing by hypnotic suggestion, which can enhance immune system functioning.

This raises the question, Whodunit? Was the healing effected by my allegedly awesome amethyst palms, or by the young woman's own immune system responding to the little laying-on-of-hands ritual we enacted? I don't know whodunit, but over the years of my clinical social work practice I utilize hypnotherapy to successfully clear up another skin rash and to eliminate a viral wart that's formed on my daughter Amy's foot. The mystery and reality of such healings remain a topic of great significance to me.

Spirit Deer (1970 and on)

I inwardly "hear" the following poem resonate from a corner near the ceiling of Marty Cohen's apartment in Buffalo, New York, Thanksgiving, 1970. I transcribe this audition word for word immediately after returning to myself :

An Unknown Totem Spoke To Me

"You will learn to understand this
about the animals:
that they give chase on rutted trails
and by night are hunted down
trails which are gores of fire.

That thirteen slain deer
on a mountainside is a song;
the drench of blood into wet moss
music slower than you can bear.
That that which is, is--
you carve a wooden image of the Dancer.
The beast runs with Her through his blood.

Among the forest you sense hidden doors.
Behind those doors we live:

39

The antler its own weapon.

The body its own larder.

The bone-heap its own marker."

Now, western Colorado, 1973: I'm visiting my cousin who lives in a tipi on his large rural acreage. As we sit outside his tipi, first peripherally, then more directly a little later on, I see a deer made of white light standing or grazing not far from us. I mention this to my cousin, who says, "You're just seeing that now? I've been watching it for fifteen minutes."

Over the years, Deer remain one of those animals I feel most en rapport with. In one dream, my daughter and I see a white-tailed deer and a complete song springs out of my mouth. Thereafter, I frequently sing it when sighting deer around our house in town or in the wild. The song begins, "Sacred Whitetail yi yi yi!" Deer invariably pause and listen intently to it. But then, deer like to be sung to. Try it sometime if you get the chance.

I also happen upon a surprising number of deer skulls and antlers. Of the five or six I come upon, the strangest episode involves walking one way along a trail in the country, then returning by the same route about twenty minutes later, and finding a deer skull in the middle of the trail. It's confounding--I see no other hikers during the course of this walk. My findings inspire another poem:

The Antlers

Began as an itch, when buds rubbed
through their green shells. I would
walk alone to a hemlock grove
and rub my head against the burly bark.
One morning, bent to a lake's face,
I saw my own, crowned with unmistakable
spikes. As suns grew warmer,
these forked forth, insignia of my place
among rooted and footed ones of the wood.

40

I am the moving forest.
When men dance, skulls adorned
with my buckdom, they may enter
my high longsight in their ecstasy
(for all dance is one).
I am the moving forest.
My headdress parts the winds.

The Man in the Blue Cape (1971)

A prelude to this tale's a dream I had in 1963, at age fourteen, before we moved from our first house in Kansas City out to staid suburbs in Shawnee Mission, on the Kansas side. In the dream, a man in a blue cape brings me to a group of young people seated around a campfire circle somewhere outside town. He tells us that he's gathered us together because he's working with "telepathic teenagers." That's all I recall of this early, nearly lucid dream.

Now, New Haven, Connecticut: While visiting a high school classmate who's a senior at Yale, I attend Easter services in a fine old church. The place is packed. There's barely room to squeeze into the crowded pew where I sit far from either aisle. After the service begins, one more person enters the church, a tall young man in a blue cape. Among all the many pews in the huge place, he picks the one I sit in, and squeezes his way down the row to wedge himself in right beside me.

I immediately feel an energy commence to pass from him to me. It's ambiguous; I'm not certain just what's happening, and I feel a natural urge to protect myself from potential psychic incursion. The energy persists, circulating from his solar plexus to mine. This is subtle but definite. After a matter of minutes, as the Easter service continues, I feel a sort of easing of the energy and the blue-caped stranger says under his breath, obviously just to me, "Okay." He then gets up, squeezes his way back down the row, and leaves the church. I never understand what's happened there.

Birdwindmindstream Transmission (1973)

En route with Leslie and a friend to Lamoni, Iowa to attend an early eco-awareness conference at Lamoni College (now called Graceland University), we stop in at a rural roadside diner. As we file in toward the booths, an old farmer is leaving with a friend. He looks closely at me as we pass, exclaims something about or to me under his breath, and the next thing I know, I have the overwhelming sense of being part of his breath, which is part of a larger more powerful wind which blows through both of us, streaming with birdsong. The two of us share a tacit eye-to-eye, and mind-to-mind connection which lifts me into an intense totemic experience of a unique and briefly bestowed birdwindmindstream transmission, direct from the fields and fencerows of his osmotic, hidden life. It's a birdy and benevolent kind of medicine. Then the old farmer passes by me and out the diner door, and that moment passes with him.

Telepathic Ten Year Old (1974)

I'm teaching five to eleven year olds at a very progressive "free school" in Kansas City. There are no grades or set classes, though we offer individualized reading and math instruction. We do all kinds of cool, fun things with the kids. I've been sharing the Zener cards used by pioneer parapsychologist J. B. Rhine to test for ESP with my students. There are 25 cards in the Zener deck, featuring 5 shapes to guess from: a circle, a plus sign, a wave sign, a square, and a star.

The ten and eleven year old girls are best. Traci gets something like eleven out of twenty-five cards right, which with a 1 in 5 per card chance of being right on a given draw, is remarkable. She's so "on," we decide to graduate to pure telepathy. I ask her to send me an image of something she really wants.

It's late afternoon, and I'm a bit drowsy. That's to my advantage, as I slip into a light sleep or trance state, and the next thing I know, I see Traci hurtling toward me in a bright orange van. The image is so lifelike and kinetic that I desperately try to get out of the way of the oncoming vehicle. Then I'm back, with no doubts: "Traci, it's an orange van and you're driving!" Up to now, Traci hasn't hesitated to tell me when my intuitions are wrong. She confirms that I got her orange van fantasy exactly right.

Sitting Ducks (1974)

On another day at the same school, we work with Bea, a beatific Eastern European immigrant conversant with Theosophy and the more contemporary teachings of Eckankar, which the American mystic and author Paul Twitchell freely adapted from the light and sound-current teachings of Kirpal Singh, and the writings of Julian Johnson, on Surat Shabd Yoga.

With Bea's guidance, we experiment with projecting consciousness outside our bodies. Again, I'm sleepy, and again it helps: I fall into a drowse and find myself, just as intended, out at the small farm Leslie and I rent near Peculiar, Missouri, a place where some mighty peculiar things happen! I'm looking at two ducks on the big pond just down the lawn from our front door. Though the pond was clear that morning when I left for my job at the free school, when I get home that afternoon, most curious about the ducks, there they are: two quackers, floating pretty much right on the spot where I'd remote-viewed them earlier that momentarily magic afternoon.

Other similar events take place over the years, including many mornings when I watch the sun rise while lying in bed with closed eyes, then get up, go to a window, open the curtains, and see the same scene.

Nerve of Bliss (1974)

Boulder, Colorado: I'm at the first-ever session of Naropa Institute, America's first-ever Buddhist University. While in a Boulder bookstore, I come upon a work of spiritual autobiography by a man named Franklin Jones (aka Bubba Free John, and by a number of other spiritual monikers over the years prior to his death in 2008). There's a remarkable photo of him on the cover of the book. This guy's got charismatic eyes. As soon as I see the photograph, I experience a golden light shining at a terminal point above the crown of my head, glowing down through the core of my body to a lower terminal point in the region of my heart. I buy the book!

Reading it that night in my dorm room, I discover that Franklin Jones describes exactly the same esoteric experience of awakened energy as I've had in the bookstore, known as the "Amrita Nadi" or "nerve of bliss." He identifies this as a unique characteristic of his realization and his transmission of that realization.

My tendency to experience central phenomenological aspects or esoteric keynotes of a given spiritual approach merely by introduction via reading alone repeats itself over and over again as the years pass. Many people have reported experiencing similar self-revelations of particular spiritual practices or phenomena, sometimes without having prior knowledge of them. Perhaps this can be explained by Carl Jung's notion of the Collective Unconscious, or Rupert Sheldrake's theory of morphic fields, or the Yogacara Buddhist concept of alayavijnana ("store-house consciousness"), or by the Theosophical idea of the akashic records, or by past life affinities. I don't know.

In the years following my epiphany in the bookstore, related experiences take place from time to time, including apparent vivid dream-encounters with Franklin Jones, and with some of his advanced students. In 2000, I become involved with a profoundly embodied spiritual approach called Waking Down in Mutuality and discover that both its founder and my primary teacher in the process were formerly students of Franklin Jones.

Blue Pearl (1974–1976)

1974, Naropa Institute: I first encounter mention of Swami Muktananda, and read one of his autobiographical works in English, The Play of Consciousness. Muktananda, one of Franklin Jones' key early teachers, is a guru whose own teacher Nityananda was purportedly a siddha--or "perfected one"--a highly realized, massive presence in human form.

Whilst reading Play of Consciousness, which describes the unfoldment of Muktananda's sadhana under Nityananda and other great teachers, I begin to see a brilliant blue pearl, both with eyes open and closed. That autumn after the summer Naropa session, it floats for long moments in front of me on the landing of the stairs in the apartment Leslie and I share in Kansas City. The pearl appears so often and with such clarity that I know I must go see Swami Muktananda in person, for its appearance is one of the central signs of spiritual development and ongoing revelation in the Siddha Yoga path he is stewarding and teaching.

Swami Muktananda teaches not only through books and discourses, but by a direct transmission of energy called "shaktipat," via the catalyzing touch or brush of a ritual peacock feather blessing-instrument, or mysteriously, over distances and absently, as in my case. But I want direct contact with the actual, physical battery-source of the liberating shaktipat energy which reading alone has initially evoked in my psyche. So I deliver a driveaway car out to the Los Angeles area, near where Swami Muktananda has gathered with disciples and others like me who have been magnetized to his potentiating energy like bees to a wide open, pollen-filled flower.

My energy is indeed amplified in his presence, coursing through my body at the merest touch of his peacock feather duster. There is further personal contact with the swami, particularly a half-hour private interview which Leslie and I have with him in Norman, Oklahoma in 1975. There we receive his blessing on our upcoming marriage. I ask him at that time, "Are you our guru?" and he answers, "No, you are each other's guru," and that turns out to be blessedly so.

Later still, we learn of Swami Muktananda's sexual improprieties, unfortunate and disenchanting off-road excursions into what we consider misconduct. By this time we've already reoriented toward other spiritual traditions and teachers aligned with more ethical, bodhisattvic behaviors. But grace works as grace will, through whatever agencies it deigns. The self-luminous blue pearl brings new spiritual momentum to my life in the mid-seventies, at a time when much emotional confusion and overwhelming change reign in my life.

Ring and Earring Miracles and Satya Sai Baba
(1975–mid 1990's)

In 1975, I meet a man from India in an antique store in Maine who shows me a leaden ring he claims was materialized by another Indian man, named Sathya Sai Baba (1926-2011). Later, I meet two other people in different settings who possess Sai Baba items-- another ring, and a box of sacred ash called "vibhuti" which is used for purposes of healing and blessing, and which supposedly refills itself whenever it is emptied.

Now in the early eighties, my attention turns again to Sai Baba as I read Professor N. Kasturi's four volume biography, or more correctly, hagiography of Sai's remarkable life. One night I'm poring over the Kasturi book, as Leslie and our kids sleep upstairs. I wonder at the miracle working power of this maybe-saint, maybe-God-man, and further wonder whether, if his powers are real, Sai Baba could demonstrate them at a distance, as he had reportedly done thousands of times before all over the globe.

I wander down the primrose path of my wonderings yet further, idly curious whether he could dematerialize my wedding ring and rematerialize it on the ring finger of my right hand. In fact, nothing like that happens, but when Leslie wakes the following morning, *her* wedding ring has mysteriously made that very migration, without her conscious knowledge of my mental question [and, in a sense, challenge] to Sai Baba. This impresses us. Nor is this all that happens, whether to impress or bless us or both: not long thereafter, Sathya Sai's image appears on one of Leslie's dangling mother of pearl earrings. We can see quite unmistakably his orange robe, and his head crowned by the black bubble of an Indian afro, all there in one deftly formed portrait. We figure we've been favored.

Though our hearts are never stirred with true devotion for him, this certainly gets and keep our attention... for awhile. A few years later, two friends who have visited Sai Baba report distressing improprieties. A decade later, my attention is drawn to many online accounts of behaviors which I cannot understand or condone; behaviors I can't conveniently stuff under my prayer rug. I write this in an understated tone, knowing that I'm very far from comprehending the whole story of what is involved here, and that there are people that I love who have tremendous love and devotion for the enigmatic guru.

Looking Back

When I turn to survey the learnings of this period of my young adulthood, I see the centrality of my relationships with spiritual teachers and friends. My first spiritual teacher Maryona introduced me to visualization practices with light and color, and suggested that brief fasts and a primarily vegetarian diet might improve my health and my receptivity to subtle energies. Chief Lightfoot Talking Eagle made me aware of the sacred wisdom legacy of Native American peoples, and affirmed my connection with Nature spirits for the first time. My friend Judy was and is one of the more compassionate beings I've ever known. Her presence brought enormous love and support into my life.

In Scotland, the Caddys, R. Ogilvie Crombie, Dorothy Maclean in particular, and others at the Findhorn Community woke me up to the incredible promise of full collaboration with the spirits of Nature. My meeting with Chogyam Trungpa at Findhorn inaugurated a closer association with Buddhism. While in Scotland, I spent a good deal of time tromping around the Highlands and some of the larger Hebridean islands, and that beautiful, beloved country permanently opened me to new nuances of color and natural energy.

While working with children at the free school in Kansas City, I began to delve more deeply into parapsychology, and was impacted by experiences of telepathy and remote viewing, which helped me gain confidence in another way of seeing and being. Such confidence can be contagious. I hope this memoir helps transmit and spread it around to more people, for we will feel more able to take on the challenges of contemporary life as we extend our sense of what is possible for ourselves.

During this time, I took an interest in the teachings of several charismatic guru-figures, and was both benefitted and ultimately made cautious by my contacts with them. These encounters alerted me to the paradoxical truth that we humans can be wise and powerful in some ways while simultaneously being quite limited by gaps in our psychological and moral development. Assimilating this lesson can save one a lot of time, confusion, and hurt.

The beginning of my lifelong partnership with Leslie Berman in 1972 was the single most significant event of my young adulthood. It is impossible to express the love and joy and warmth and growth she has brought into my life.

This period as a whole was the beginning of a prolonged pilgrimage into myself, and outward into the wide world and the lives of others. These inward and outward journeys left me more sensitive to the possibilities of connection and productive cooperation with other people and the kingdoms of Nature. I hope these accounts and the poems that accompany them convey something of the intimacy with the land that developed as I navigated about from place to place. And I hope they will inspire readers to cultivate their own cooperative communion with the land and its material and subtle inhabitants, in order to serve the earth.

IV. A Time of Travel

Guidance for the Solstice (1975)

After getting married in April, 1975, Leslie and I begin a period of travel. We've stayed for two weeks at the Findhorn Community in Scotland, and soon we plan to leave. I sit down in the Sanctuary there to request inner guidance about the next step in our journey, and hear the "still small voice" within say that we could go to the holy island of Lindisfarne (located off the east coast of northern England) for Summer Solstice.

This is the first time I've consciously sought guidance and received it clearly from that still, small voice, which sounds like my own voice speaking from the center of my chest; that "daimonion," (literally, "divine something") which Socrates refers to in Plato's account of the "Apology of Socrates" as an inner intelligence which guides, and advises against making harmful mistakes: "This sign I have had ever since I was a child. The sign is a voice which comes to me and always forbids me to do something which I am going to do, but never commands me to do anything..." (Plato's "Apology of Socrates", English translation by Benjamin Jowett.) My experience tallies with that of Socrates: the messages I receive from my daimonion are always respectful of my free will to decide on a course of action, with the infrequent exception of times when my inner voice alerts me about a course of action which would be downright dangerous or foolish for me to pursue. Then the message I receive can be emphatically forbidding, as in "Don't do this!"

We travel south from Findhorn to Lindisfarne. After visiting the remains of the monastery established by St. Aidan there around 635 A.D., and getting pleasantly smashed on mead at a nearby pub, we rest in our bed and breakfast room. I fall asleep and wake as dusk darkens the island. Mist swims a spit of land that recedes down the beach to pounding surf I can hear through our second story window. Impelled out into the dimming day, I head toward the mist-thick beach. A group of seven figures emerges from the fog, and as they walk toward me I see they're wearing monk's robes with hooded cowls. There's an inevitability about the scene. I feel no surprise, more a sense that whatever this is, it's what I came here for.

I meet the hooded group, who are flesh and blood contemporary persons, not spectral phantom monks from the pre-medieval abbey on the island. They barely speak, but one tells me they've come from Edinburgh to meditate at Summer Solstice. I'm instantly accepted into a group of people who carry an extraordinary aura of silence and shared purpose. We walk to an ancient graveyard within hearing of the swaying tidal roar, and sit among the graves to meditate in a stillness that soon eclipses everything, even as night falls and completely obliterates us, merging our meditating bodies, leaning gravestones, the windswept sky, and my downshifting mind into one single sable field of pure black presence.

After a timeless interval, I rise and wordlessly depart the group, which seems to be set like a midnight-black diamond in the heart of silence. This silence stays alive and strong in me as I make my way back to my young wife resting in our bed and breakfast room on Lindisfarne.

Bathed in Grace (1975)

On a bus from Oxford to London with my wife. I'm feeling wretched because we've recently fought. She's quiet and forlorn. Suddenly, I'm enveloped in glory and Light. Nothing subtle--this is full-out beatitude, and I intuitively know it's being triggered by a source outside my psyche. I further somehow know that that source is someone seated somewhere behind me. There's an element of embarrassment in all this for me--to have behaved so badly and madly with Leslie, yet to be held in such a state of grace feels like a vulnerable exposure. In his Poems of Innocence and Experience, William Blake wrote that "we are put on Earth a little space/That we may learn to bear the beams of love." The bus bears us toward London. The love never lets up. It fills and eventually settles and soothes me.

When we arrive and are about to disembark, I know I must wait for passengers behind me to file out, so I can finally see the person who's held me in such vast, beatified awareness. And sure enough, here she comes: a frail old grey-haired lady. I simply know she's the one. She passes my seat without any kind of acknowledgement, and I maneuver myself into line right behind her. As she starts down the bus's brief, steep stairway to the pavement, I watch her waver slightly. The climb down is a chore for her old body. My body is still so charged up from our mysterious encounter (a "God-appointment" to be sure) that it's possible for me to project a ray of energy from my solar plexus to hold and steady her as she descends the stairs. She stands a moment on the station pavement then turns around, beams brightly up at me, says "Thank you," and is on her way.

Vision of Reverent Hands (1975)

I fall into a heavy, buzzy afternoon slumber in the spiritually charged realm of Glastonbury, England. Leslie and I have just visited the Chalice Well, the lofty Tor, and the ancient Glastonbury Abbey, some buried parts of which were rediscovered thanks to information provided in seances by a long-deceased monk associated with the place.

I find myself witness to a lucid dream-vision of reverent, venerable hands pausing and passing over rectangular shapes draped by white linens fringed with intricate lacework. This vision is completely perplexing to me, but it carries the felt sense of some archaic, repetitive, numinous activity. Something sacred has been inscribed on silence in this place.

Less than a month later, we land on the holy Isle of Iona, off the west coast of Scotland. While Leslie relaxes at our bed and breakfast there, I attend a Communion at the Iona Abbey. I'm curious to witness what is described in a brochure as an historically authentic traditional Communion. Expecting a tray of thin eucharistic wafers to be brought in, I am surprised to see rectangular loaves of fresh-baked bread draped by white linens with fine lace fringe borne in and placed upon the altar. The priest's hands lift the lacey linens, and my puzzling Glastonbury vision makes intense sense as we break the body of the fragrant loaf, and taste.

This kind of visionary window seems to open on the collective soul-life of the country as we continue along our way. I try to write about what I see and sense, albeit uncertain of the degree to which true vision is alloyed by the workings of my lively imagination:

There's More "When" Here

They lovingly maintain their thatched and oak-beamed cottages, where the dense energy of generations amasses.

The fields here are often very *seen*. In certain valleys even shadows seem more deeply sentient, somehow wakened under the gaze of ages of eyes from those of Pict to Celt to centurion to Saxon to those of the village lout or poet.

The country fairly froths with contemplation and plumes of Being that rise from churchyards with their giant yews and gray, lichened graves.

Astral temples stand in many groves and glens, tall bastions of Druidic attention and intention reinforced by later prayers and workings of the rural faithful and their elemental and angelic co-workers.

Telluric currents of elven, gnomish, and faerie consciousness run under the earth, gathering in reservoirs or vortices in subterranean caves; emerging on moors, near barrows and megalithic stones.

Communion with the countryside looms up like an aesthetic cumulous from the otherwise rather flat, repressed English sensibility, arising tumescent in the form of rowdy festivals and rustic fairs, gnarly balladry, wild convoluted poems and plays and dances, and the sublime viney curvilinear meanderings of Celtic art and instrumental music.

The tangled profusion of Celtic design: lines fold back on themselves in interknit geometries wherein nest birds and bears and men. Our eyes exhaust themselves, after trying to attend to these unwinding lines. Then the Mind's Eye opens.

The landscape's stacked and stratified with layers of history, and ancient heartfelt awareness striates the inscape with enduring ley lines that link sacred sites. There's more "when" here.

The Old Ones (1975)

I realize that for some readers this entry will register high on the Woo-Woo Scale of Improbability. However, like many individuals before me over the centuries, I've sensed beings from a parallel realm while visiting certain places in the U.K., and the U.S.. Known by many names, including the "faery folk" or the "Sidhe" in Ireland and Scotland, these beings seem to be quite different from the more diminutive, gossamer fairies of familiar fairy tales. However, the dissimilar spellings can be confusing, because these two words are frequently used interchangeably to denote both the small, aerial flower fairies and the more formidable, subterranean Sidhe. In this book, the word "fairy" is used to specify the former and "faery" the latter beings. If my intuitions are at all accurate, the faery folk are powerful, watchful, elusive, exalted, and wise. I wonder how one of them would characterize us humans? The following poems are descriptive reports, and gestures of connection made to an ancient race:

Glimpses of Faeryland

We check in at an bed and breakfast near Mellaray Abbey, below the Knocknealdown Mountains of southern Ireland.

After sinking into the first deep waters of sleep, I return to my identity. I'm standing on an immense gloomy stone stairway, surrounded by mossy walls of unseen height. I have no idea where my sleeping body lies, I'm so carried away, into a realm as real as this waking one and more, for in my translocation this seems to be the only moment that has ever been.

Now I'm drawn down the stairs through a percipient, not-unfriendly darkness and suddenly come upon a marvel-ous city of silver domed dwellings with intricate curlicues

and designs upon them. Silver horns and moons curve upward from the roofs.

This is certainly not my place. I find it very difficult to
return to form. After a minute or so of trying, I have to call
on my spiritual protectors to draw me bodyward again.
Passing through a conflagration of great winds, I fly up the
tunnel back to our bed and breakfast room where my nap-
ping body lies, and slowly lower down into my flesh.

Years later, I read in a book of Irish lore that the underground Hall of the Queen of the Faeries is said to be located
at the foot of the Knocknealdown Mountains, precisely the
site of that bed and breakfast place. In retrospect, I think I
may have glimpsed the fabled"faery city under the mountain," as convincing as our own reality, yet so conclusively
OTHER.

As we travel on through Britain, I sometimes receive diapha-
nous impressions of faery energy, such as this one:

The Old Ones

(Wales)

A talkative fire--
lamb and bird sounds
blur on the wind.
High shale cliffs
front the valley's east slope.
Breeze brushes
over poplar there.
Raven lofts
over hallucinated walls
of stacked fieldstone.
Two roads wind away west
toward old blunt peaks.

Now
we're taken in--
peripheral, nearly
parallel us,
light fey eyes open
into our moment--
Old Ones view us.
Our circles grow near.
They send a night moth.
They summon and bless.

Vibratory Night Near Sparta (1975)

Greece: Leslie and I rent a car and drive from Athens to the Peloponnesian Peninsula. We stop in a remote mountainous region above the ancient site of the city of Sparta. There's a bright full sweep of stars. We get out of the car to rest and relieve ourselves. The entire earth is vibrating at a low but quite audible frequency.

There are no visible towers or power stations, no human habitations, no artificial lights, no other traffic on the highway. The hum deepens; the earth itself seems super-sentient. The vibration comes up through the soles of our feet and legs direct from the soil, which feels to us as if suffused with a dense, magnetic energy. It's like we've stepped into another dimension, a more highly resonant realm.

Now the energy continues to lift and the bass buzz becomes more audible. As this happens our own bodies take on a more charged, bioelectronic quality. Silence deepens in our minds like a reservoir fills with water after heavy rain. We stay until it feels like it's time to go, then drive away into the night, our bodies full of sparkling darkness, like the star-fields floating overhead.

"Mark's Gone Back to Rest in Jesus for Awhile" (1975)

Somewhere in Europe, in a dream, I hear the words, "Mark's gone back to rest in Jesus for awhile," set to a gospel music melody. This is clearly a reference to my friends Larry and Alice and their extremely strange psychedelic spiritual teacher Mark, and it makes me wonder whether maybe Larry and Alice have had a change of heart and left Mark's fold for that of the Good Shepherd.

Other possible interpretations, like Mark himself becoming a Christian, seem unlikely. The one time I sat in a circle with him when he visited Kansas City, I found the man to be frightening. He spoke and gazed at us penetratingly, and demonstrated an alarming plasticity of physical movement, especially very odd, exaggerated facial contortions I wouldn't care to ever witness again. No, Mark seemed to bear an energy antithetical to Christlike love, and I didn't trust him.

So, waking from the dream, I hope that something has changed for my friends and that they've moved on to greener spiritual pastures. Sure enough, on our return to Kansas City after the European journey which also was our honeymoon, Leslie and I visit Larry and Alice. I'd written them a letter chronicling the brief dream-song, and they meet us with the joyous announcement that they've jettisoned that dark old Mark and turned to Jesus. Larry then proceeds to sing us a gospel song he wrote after his conversion experience, which happened as he sat beneath a walnut tree. As far as I know, my friends have remained devout Christians to this day, secure in the worship of the God of their understanding.

Karmu Karma (1975)

Cambridge, Massachusetts: Leslie and I visit the Boston area and sleep on the floor of a house of old friends of mine while there. When living in Kansas City in 1974, we'd each seen a chiropractor. Leslie's spine was x-rayed in his office, revealing a serious, chronic misalignment, the kind that doesn't change overnight, or even altogether ever. Mindful of this, and of other health issues, we decide to go see a famous healer named Karmu during our visit.

Karmu, an automobile mechanic, root doctor, and spiritual

healer from the Caribbean, has for many years conducted healing sessions out of his apartment, also dispensing dark, odiferous herbal elixirs and singing along to recordings of self-composed music. Bare chested, powerful, unpredictable, and wild, Karmu is a force of Nature.

He lays hands on Leslie's back, then after doing some housecleaning for him in his funky apartment, we return to my friends' house and eventually bed down on their floor for the night. Leslie falls asleep first. Resting alertly awake beside her, I hear an enormous "crack" which seems to come from her back. We're lying on an old wood floor, and I discount the possibility of such a loud sound coming from her back as she lies there in motionless slumber. Surely it has to be the floor beneath us creaking. But the "crack" resounds again, clearly from inside Leslie's body. I note this with astonishment, and when we wake in the morning, I share the story with her.

Within a year's time, Leslie again sees a chiropractor. We bring in her x-ray from 1974, and learn that her chronic misalignment has inexplicably self-corrected by 90%. Her spine is almost normal, and has become even more so in the decades since that crucial crack.

Hitching a Ride on Sant Mat Sound Currents (1976)

Burney, California: I'm sleeping next to Leslie at the Polarity Health Lodge where she's pursuing an intensive nine week accreditation course in Polarity Balancing massage, nutrition, and yoga. The folks who teach the course and run the Lodge all walk a particular Eastern path called Sant Mat, in which initiated meditators follow a practice that involves increasing at-one-ment with transcendental Light and a subtle "current" of sound.

As I slip into the deeper waters of sleep, I somehow enter this sound current, which surges like a jetstream in a riverine band that spans the planet. My consciousness is carried along, above mountain ranges, high isolated temples, deserts, watercourses, and other scenes, before I wake up grateful and amazed. It's evident to me that I've somehow hitched a ride on the sound current these Sant Mat Polarity folks travel in their subtle vehicles as a regular spiritual practice.

Silent Compliment (1977)

Athens, Georgia: I'm working at the local Economic Opportunity Agency (EOA) while also studying for an Masters in Social Work degree at the University of Georgia. One misty, moisty morning, several EOA employees and I are filing into the offices there. In front of me in line is a slender young woman in an attractive summer dress. I'm just a little too shy to say, "Nice dress" out loud, not knowing her well and still being somewhat inward in a just-woke-not-long-ago way, but the words pass clearly through my mind. She turns and says, out loud, "Thank you."

Water Spirit Chant (1977)

Near Athens, Georgia at an outdoor fair: It's an overcast morning, and I'm walking about with my guitar, picking notes that somehow correspond to who I see and what I feel as I stroll around the fairgrounds. Those clouds up there look fat with rain. I launch into Jim Pepper's water spirit chant "Witchi Tai To," which he adapted from a ceremonial song he learned from his Comanche grandfather. At the chant's first few words, a light rain lets go liquid arrows from the vast cloud-bow above us. I don't want it to rain on the crowd, so I stop chanting and playing right away. The rain stops exactly when I stop. It's instantaneous and definite. I'm tempted to repeat the sequence, but don't want to play with Power.

The rain never returns; the cloudy cover lifts and sun prevails over the fair. Such synchronicities may be sheer chance, but the immediate way the rain started and stopped with my music makes this event quite memorable. I still go out and ululate Jim Pepper's prayerful chant in times of August drought.

Golden Opportunity (1978)

Athens, Georgia: We live communally in a farmhouse at the edge of town. There's a sloping field, and a grove of old beech trees a few hundred feet from the house. Right outside the front door is a big dead tree. That tree itself is a story: one morning in autumn I wake and walk outside to see it completely covered with fluttering orange leaves. Startled, I look again more closely, and see that the leaves are actually a giant migratory "kaleidoscope" (aka, a "rabble" or "swarm") of monarch butterflies, using the tree as a rest stop on their long way south to Mexico.

A good many energetic, telepathic, and other mysterious events happen in and around that farmhouse during the two years we live there.

One night in late spring, while Leslie meets inside the house with her women's group, I lay out in a hammock in a little stand of trees beside the slanting field a stone's throw from our house. There's a deepening awareness of my belly, and increasing relaxation, as the hammock sways me like a cradle. I sink into an odd receptive state.

I hear a baby cry three times from my belly, and assume I'm hearing me--a body memory. Next, I experience my auric field rotating horizontally, in relation to the earth, and clockwise. I can distinctly feel the forms of the women in Leslie's group, as my huge distended field rotates through the room where they sit talking.

A little later, the group lets out. As they come out the front door and head towards their cars, one woman nears the hammock a little and calls out in my direction, "I'm glad you remembered!"

About ten years later, during a session of neo-Reichian psychotherapy involving deep, rhythmic breathing, I relive what seem to be visceral memories of my first such experience of auric rotation, which happened sometime during a traumatic six-week period of touch deprivation following my birth. I try to convey these experiences in a poem:

First Memories

(Of Premature Birth)

I've watched my tumble from her
from a lucid witness place above my head.
I've heard my own birth cries well up

from my groaning grown-up guts.
People in a semi-circle stand above us,
white masks over their mouths and noses.
I hear my breathing, alone
for the first time.
My auric field dilates. From my bright incubator,
I scan through walls in an extended clockwise sweep.
I trace through moving bodies for the one
that might approach and hold me close.
Hands come and fold the starched white
linens at right angles, with brisk care.
Sometimes they dip and pick me up.
I sink in and out of sleep despite the glare.

But back to that enchanted Georgia night: I continue to shift into a more expanded state of consciousness. At some point, I get up out of the hammock, and walk into the moonlit beech grove. A small spherical golden light appears around eighteen inches in front of me, at chest level. I look for but cannot see the firefly that I assume emits it. There is no bug, no explanation for this lucid light. So I reverently bow, with hands joined in front of my heart, as in the Eastern greeting, "Namaste." At this, the light nears and glows magnetically at the tips of my joined fingers. I bow again, astounded. The light draws closer yet, I bow again, and suddenly it plunges into my chest, bearing a delicious warmth and buoyancy. I rest rapt for a moment, then the orb departs, seemingly quite alive, hovering before me for a moment then disappearing. Never to be forgotten.

Other lights and prodigies appear there in that place, sometimes also seen by friends, but this event remains singular in my experience as an especially nurturing and golden opportunity.

"We're Looking This Place Over for a Friend" (1978)

Mt. Hood Wilderness Area, east of Portland, Oregon: I'm driving through the back country toward a small lake I've intuitively chosen to be the site of my first three day vision quest. I bring along only some water to drink and a little tobacco to smoke and pray with once each evening. There's no traffic for many miles, but as I near the lake, a white VW Bug with two young women in it appears right behind me. When I arrive, they do too. As I select a place to put up my pup tent, they circumambulate the lake without a word to me. Yet I sense a possible connection of some kind.

I'm getting settled in my camp, staking out a square of ground in line with the Four Directions, a square I'll never leave for three long days. The two young women finally pass in front of me and regard me solemnly. I ask them if they're going to camp here at the lake, but they say no, "We're looking this place over for a friend of ours who's going to camp here". That's all they say, and then they leave. Somehow I feel supported, even blessed.

Three days pass. Very little happens, as far as I'm aware. At one point, as I shelter from the summer sun inside my little tent, a mole scurries over the slope of tent fabric just above my head. I count this as a possible totemic encounter... I'm just not sure. I'm doing this without the proper guidance and the supportive prayers of a qualified medicine person, which is not recommended. However, I gradually "arrive" a bit more, feeling light and refined from fasting, and quite present.

Now the vision quest's about to end. It's been so hot and dry, and I yearn for a final, more definitive sign, so I ask the Great Spirit, "If it's Your will, let clouds cover the sun." Clouds rush in to shroud the sun in minutes, for the first time that day.

I still can't quite compute the unlikely beginning of this quest: a vast wilderness area, with many such small lakes and no cars until the two young women come along and seemingly accompany me at the outset of my sojourn. I never see another soul the entire time I'm there.

Spirit on the Water (1978)

At the edge of Oregon wilderness, we're about to hit the trail to our campsite. Our friend Jim's been here before--he's a native Oregonian. As we stand near the trailhead at the edge of the forest, a large butterfly lights directly on Jim's hand. I sense a welcoming presence, one Jim may have met up with before on previous visits to this remote place. We pause for a timeless span of time, then forge ahead on down the trail.

At a broad, gushing creek....a place of two forks meeting. I remember rapids and little 'water stumbles' less steep than waterfalls. Wonderful sounds accompany the creek as it skeedaddles over boulders, chilly current glugging 'round their contours. There are other underwater sounds as well, like the grating of big rocks jostled by fast-flashing water, and the submerged burps of current in contact with certain boulders below the creek's turbulent surface.

Late afternoon: fantastic cold immersions; long leanings into the cold, cold stream. Letting go of urban energy, we relax together as day dims. Shadows lengthen as light recedes down the winding creek valley.

"The Valley Spirit Never Dies"

(line from chapter 6, the Tao te Ching)

Listen to wave curls holding
in the clear current.
This canyon where sound becomes voices.

Rite of suns
disappearing down the steep
creek valley. Birds attend.

Now a light blue orb hovers over a burbling little water-stumble. Jim and I see it and share our perceptions, which as I recall the three women with us do not share. We watch the blue orb float about 20 feet away from where we sit. It stays there for some time, then as daylight dies away altogether, it's finally no longer visible. But Jim and I feel met yet again.

"What is Her Real Name?" (1978)

Lichen Intentional Community, near Wolf Creek, Oregon: We sleep in a tiny geodesic dome in a forest of tall douglas fir and stocky cedar trees. Warmed by a little pot-bellied wood stove, we also have one stool, a narrow bed, a kerosene lamp, and outside a hundred feet away, a self-constructed outhouse. That's about it. We're happy.

One night as Leslie sleeps, I gaze deep into her peaceful face, silently wondering, "Who is she, really? What is her real name?" Leslie's a quiet sleeper, but immediately after that last unspoken question, she says clearly out loud, "Pb-----," a name I've certainly never heard. She's completely quiet the rest of that silent, holy night.

A poem from that period describes our strange, serene communication:

Your True Name

With you in a round room
where you pronounce your true name
aloud in your sleep in response
to my silent request.

Peaceful in here...shaggy cedars
are white bells.
Your gentle eyebrows fringe
the edge of snowy groves.

Over the following years, this happens many times, always according to a similar pattern: I spontaneously pose a mental question as Leslie slumbers. The question isn't addressed to her, but to myself about some matter of importance I'm considering. Then, within a moment, Leslie "answers" the question verbally, often with a binary yes-no response, but sometimes with a pertinent phrase. Her response almost always provides a helpful perspective.

Looking Back

I smile as I think back on this time of travel, which ushered in new awareness of the subtle energies to be encountered in wilderness and more urban settings. The inner and outer act of pilgrimage is a time-honored way to connect with the living energies of the earth. Outwardly, one makes a physical journey to a place of power in a reverent state, mindful of meaningful signs and synchronicities along the way. Inwardly, one attunes to the energetically quickening qualities of natural power spots like the ocean, certain mountains, groves, and springs; or to the blessing-force of spiritually charged religious communities, shrines, temples, stupas, and the like. Already aware of the transformative possibilities of pilgrimage from my earlier travels in Scotland and the U.S., I continued to discover how this attitude toward travel can facilitate our ability to absorb, benefit from, and even to bless and enhance the energy of such sites.

Leslie and I had great fun roaming through Europe and especially in the British Isles, where from time to time I experienced the opening of visionary windows which provided insight into the soul-life of the land, and the way in which generation after generation of human history persists here as a kind of living strata, which can be accessed through dreams, or active imagination, or suddenly and spontaneously. I think a lot of people can relate to this--it's not unusual to sense great peace in one location, for example, or something distressed or distressing in another.

We all have some latent or active capacity to sense those places where environmental harmony has been disrupted by a history of war, oppression, or pollution. In sharing my stories, I want to affirm our ability to intuit the atmosphere and attributes of the places we visit and abide in. We can all bless these places with our love.

Leslie and I lived communally for most of time we spent in Athens, Georgia, where I got my Masters in Social Work degree. While there, I worked as a community organizer with folks in four rural counties, and often took refuge from this intense work by visiting a nearby grove of beech trees and on camping trips with friends. These intimate meetings with Nature helped open me to inner wisdom and direction.

We each have our own special ways to connect with Nature and access inner guidance. I'd be delighted if these tales of travel spark readers to take an inventory of their unique ways of getting in touch with the natural world, and with the wise guidance of that "divine something" in us all.

V. Mostly Home in Arkansas

("You'll find your happiness lies right under your eyes,
back in your own backyard."
--from the song "Back in Your Own Backyard"
by Al Jolson, Billy Rose, and Dave Dryer)

The Knee of Healing (1979)

Fayetteville, Arkansas: I'd injured my right knee by running without a proper warm up when Leslie and I visited Crater Lake the past summer. It remains sore, so I go to an orthopedist, and am told that my right lateral meniscus is torn. I'm advised to receive surgery. Instead, I contact the Chirotheisian Church, a California group that for many years has offered prayers for healing with a good track record of success. The lady I reach on the phone suggests I lie down at the same time in the afternoon for seven consecutive afternoons, and rest as the church's prayer team concentrates on my healing. On at least three of these afternoons, I feel a nimbus of energy surround my entire body, then zero in around my right knee cap and stay there for a minute or two.

After this week, I'm able to bend my knee with less and less discomfort, and it eventually heals altogether, given patient attention to avoid reinjury, and the regular practice of a Taoist self-massage technique a healer teaches me: Sit comfortably with knees bent. Rub your palms together and clap your hands a few times to warm them up. Then rotate your left and right palms around your left and right kneecaps, warmly massaging clockwise around both kneecaps in a steady, attentive, unhurried, soothing way, circling them forty-nine times. I still do this old Taoist practice more days than not, and my knees are just fine.

I Sing Grandma Out to Sea (1979)

Our first spring in Arkansas: I'm a VISTA volunteer in Ft. Smith, working as a community organizer. I sleep on a mat on the floor of an older home there. One night I "wake" into a lucid dream: I'm in my grandmother Helen Oelsner's apartment in Kansas City. My brother sits wordlessly and somehow not fully consciously on her bed. Grandma and I are standing. We're looking deep into each other's eyes--soul deep--and I'm singing her a song in a language I don't know (Glossolalia--that is, speaking in tongues? The Hebrew of her youth?). The song's about setting sail on the great cosmic ocean. A stream of deep communion and what feels like blessing flows through the two of us, then I wake up in the darkened Ft. Smith house, and have to get up to go to the bathroom. While briefly up, I check my watch and note the time.

In the morning, I'm wakened by a phone call from my parents. They've called to break the news that Grandma died last night. Before they can say the time, I ask them if it was around the time I'd had that dream, and yes, it happened just exactly then. My folks don't seem to register this when I tell them, at least not consciously. I'd never dreamt of Grandma before this, as far as I can recall.

Two memories tag along behind this one. First, during my junior year at the University of Aberdeen in Scotland, Grandma comes to visit me. As she sits with me in the Marcliff Hotel in Aberdeen, I experience a subtle but distinct crack of expansion in a suture in my skull approximate to my 3rd eye, then a clockwise swirling of energy there. It seems somehow linked to, or even brought about by, Grandma's gentle presence. And second, during my subsequent senior year in college at Oberlin, I meet Griscom Morgan from Antioch College (his father Arthur founded Antioch, and was chairman and a manager of the massive Tennesse Valley Authority project).

An older man with substantial spiritual roots, Griscom invites my participation as an organizer in an educational project to help preserve rural Ohio school systems from mass consolidations. In the course of our conversations, we speak about being able to assist family members and others make the transition at death. I ask him what to do to help dying family members, and he turns to me with great intensity and says, "When the time comes, you will *know* just what to do."

I get goose bumps from above my head all the way down into my scalp when I recall this conversation with Griscom. His transmission of soul-force and the confidence with which he spoke very likely helped to plant in me the seeds of deep awareness I would later need to help facilitate my grandmother's free and peaceful passage from this world into the post-mortem realms.

67

"You Could Work on a Book About Natural Means of Protecting People from Radiation If You Want To" (1980)

It's a hot summer day and I've spent much of it outdoors on our forty wild acres near Kingston, Arkansas. Now I'm standing meditatively inside our little hexagonal cabin, when suddenly, a group of figures composed of white light appear within the field of white light which vibrates in and around me. I hear this unexpected message coming from them: "You could work on a book about natural means of protecting people from radiation if you want to."

The wording of the message is completely respectful of my free will. The sacredness and clarity of the moment is so memorable that I recall it several weeks later when Steven Schechter, N.D., a naturopathic physician, shows up on our land unannounced. He tells me that he is just beginning research on a pamphlet about natural means of protecting the body from ionizing radiation. We end up working together for over seven years on what is finally published in 1988 as a full-length book titled <u>Fighting Radiation with Foods, Herbs, and Vitamins</u>. It appears in two more editions over the next several years, further expanded by Steve, the primary author, to include some information about counteracting the effects of chemical pollutants.

In an appendix to the book, we include a shortened version of a longer essay I have written, "Unorthodox Approaches to Radiation Protection Deserving of Further Research." The essay begins:

> While collecting data on radiation protection, we came upon a number of unorthodox, speculative approaches to the subject which might further a shift toward more holistic research and treatment in this field. We found that research with promising implications for radiation protection has been conducted by experts in areas of study as varied as allopathic medicine, naturopathy, homeopathy, crystallography, bacteriology, parapsychology, and psychoneuroimmunology (the study of how emotional states and mental attitudes affect the immune system). This survey presents those findings which we consider to have the most potential for radiation protection.

A longer form of this essay is available to interested readers, who may contact me through my website. One unpublished portion of it antedates and has helped inspire a current endeavor, the Psi-Sci Alliance project described in the story "How the Hell Did I Do That? (1998 and 2010)" later in these pages.

While writing the essay, I encounter a book called Psychic Archeology by Jeffrey Goodman, Ph.D., which contains the first references I have seen to gifted intuitives collaborating with investigatory researchers. When working on his master's thesis at the University of Arizona, Goodman made an important archeological finding with information supplied by a psychic named Aron Abrahamsen. Abrahamsen was able to predict the site of a successful dig down to the exact ten foot square of earth to excavate, the artifacts that would be found there, and at what depth they would be discovered, with 78% accuracy--eighteen out of twenty-three correct predictions.

In his book, Dr. Goodman gives a fascinating account of the use of psychics in nineteenth and twentieth century archeological research. With his assistance, I contact Mr. Abrahamsen and arrange to send him nine questions about facets of radiation protection. Though overly generalized, his responses are interesting enough to lead me to consider future cooperative ventures with intuitives. The Psi-Sci Alliance involves such an initiative, linking psychics with scientists in an attempt to generate effective methods of mitigating climate change.

In the years since the book on radiation protection was published, I have occasionally received specific intuitive guidance alerting me to opportunities to undertake particular projects for the sake of human and environmental well-being. The Psi-Sci Alliance is one of these projects. While working on it, I am experiencing the same consistent flow of synchronicities--books and contacts all arriving in perfect timing to support my work on the project--which I also delighted in as I helped Steve research, edit, and write parts of our book on radiation protection.

These are examples of moving from the stage of receiving guidance, a dream, or a vision, on to the phase of manifesting that which has been received in the material world. Robert Moss' book Dreamways of the Iroquois: Honoring the Secret Wishes of the Soul presents information he received from his dreams and scholarly research about the way people of the Mohawk Iroquois tribal culture have enacted important dreams in order to reclaim power, knowledge, and healing. We have all experienced acting on an intuitive hunch, but we don't yet have the kind of cultural permission to validate and actualize our inspirations and dreams in the same potent, often ceremonial and communal ways the Iroquois and other tribal groups have done. In my experience, the more inner permission we have to "make our dreams come true," the more interesting and productive our lives become.

A Frightful Light in the Forest (1980)

Relatively few of my non-ordinary experiences have been scary. This one happens at the hillside homestead where Leslie and I live for a time near Kingston, Arkansas. For some months we both occasionally glimpse a sphere of yellow light traveling through the trees as dusk comes on. We see a brief trajectory of radiance, more orb-like than the characteristic long rays cast by last lingering sun. Not knowing whether it's a natural phenomenon like some trick of the light through the trees, or a more arcane manifestation, we simply note it.

One warm evening well after dark, as Leslie sleeps I lie out on the wooden deck that juts over a slope fronting miles of forest. I observe the rapid advent of something strange--there's a subtle stirring in the air, but no sound or wind to speak of. I feel some force approaching, encroaching. And with that feeling comes bright light, evenly illuminating every leaf on every tree. No cars can come down our mud-rutted road without announcing their presence by bumps and engine-hum, and this light doesn't resemble headlight beams anyway. It's comprehensive, lighting up the whole area. It's coming from the north and getting brighter by the moment.

I'm apprehensive. I briefly wonder if I'm experiencing some kind of massive third eye opening, then realize that my Ajna chakra, when open to transcendental radiance--what Quakers call the "Inner Light"--does *not* have the property of illuminating an entire acre or so of pitch black forest! Now I'm more than nervous; I'm scared. I intuitively close my eyes as whatever the source of the light is approaches the deck. I feel it, somehow receiving an impression of a vibratory craft which is controlled by at least two tall, translucent beings. But of course this may all be "Close En-counters of the Third Kind" sci-fi fantasy, because my eyes are as closed as they're ever going to be--clamped shut--to avoid see-ing something utterly "other" and unspeakably eldritch; something which I fear could take control of my mind and leave me traumatized.

As I lie there rigid with fright, I focus every iota of my attention on Guru Padmasambhava's great mantra, OM AH HUM VAJRA GURU PADME SIDDHI HUM, the ancient Tibetan Buddhist invo-cation which has for years provided a protective spiritual focus for me in times of need or danger. After several tense minutes reciting the mantra, I barely lift the lid on one eye and see that the forest has returned to its blessed darkness, unstirred by whatever inau-dible whir or vibration has just departed. Shaken, I finally rise and make my way into the little six-sided cabin where Leslie sleeps, oblivious to all this High Strangeness.

Star Portals (1980)

I take a nap, and experience a complete dislocation (or reloca-tion) of my point of view: I'm in a formless state in space, looking at the starry concourse through the "gate" of two stars which I intuitively sense to be somewhere in the region of the Pleiades (the Seven Sisters). Subsequently, I pass through a series of six "clicks," like slides changing in a slide projector, in which I peer through star portals at six more different, distant yet distinct points of view, a total of seven "perches" or vantage points in space. The feeling-tone of my experience becomes more and more sublime with each successive viewing, .

A week or so later, I'm in the Fayetteville Library and hap-pen to check out Henri Corbin's great phenomenological religious study, The Man of Light in Iranian Sufism. I'm surprised to come upon a passage that describes the visions of a Sufi mystic named Ruzbehan of Shiraz (writing in 1209 A.D). He is quoted:

> Then, I concentrated my attention on the constella-tion of the Bear [*Ruzebehan is referring to the constellation Ursa Minor here, according to Corbin*] and I observed that it formed seven apertures through which God was showing himself to me. My God! I cried, what is this? He said to me: "These are the seven apertures of the throne". . . Every

71

night, I continued afterwards to observe these apertures in Heaven. . . and lo! one night I saw that they were open, and I saw the Divine Being manifesting to me through these apertures. He said to me, "I manifest to you through these openings; they form....thresholds (corresponding to the seven principal stars of the constellation) leading to the threshold of the angelic pleroma (malakut). And behold I show myself to you through all of them at once."

The constellation Ursa Minor (the Little Bear) is familiarly known as the Little Dipper because its seven brightest stars form a ladlelike shape. Although I construe the locus of my own experience to be the Pleiades, I am struck by the remarkable correspondence between these two viewings through seven star-apertures, which happen almost eight hundred years and many thousands of miles apart.

Seven years after this star portal episode, I come upon the traditional Cherokee (Tsalagi) teaching of the Seven Dancers. In her book Voices of Our Ancestors, Cherokee spiritual teacher Dhyani Ywahoo identifies the seven brightest stars or dancers of the Pleiades star system as the original home of the Tsalagi, and affirms that these seven "gates" relate to energies within us, and constitute "doorways" through our minds and hearts.

The Findhorn Community, Dorothy Maclean, and Attunement in the Ozarks (1980)

In The Findhorn Garden, one can read many communications Dorothy Maclean received from the "devas" of different plants, and of other natural forces and beings. In her introduction to these, Dorothy writes:

> Every plant does have a unique ensouling presence. These messages, however, have not been communicated by individual plants but rather by the overlighting intelligence and spirit--the deva--for each plant species. While the devas themselves are beyond form, yet are they responsible for the most precise and minute forms we behold in the plant kingdom, the wonderful exactness of each seed and leaf and blossom.

"Early Spring Evening"
(An Ozark vista by Robert Sudlow, 1970. Original oil painting in color.)

The Findhorn Garden features a photo of me and some other fellows making a big batch of compost according to specific instructions Dorothy received from what people at the community have called "the Landscape Angel, " a vast intelligence permeating the area. That was a very tangible hands-on experience of collaboration with Nature, to be sure!

Connecting with the devas through the receptive process of attunement, Dorothy and other folks at Findhorn co-created powerful links with Nature which improved soil quality and accelerated plant growth. For those interested, a self-study module which includes audios of Dorothy reading her Deva Messages and "The Doorway Process" can be purchased at the Lorian Association website.

In her book, <u>To Hear the Angels Sing: An Odyssey of Co-creation with the Devic Kingdom</u> , Dorothy elaborates on her relationship with the devas, and offers more messages; verbal 'translations' of impressions she originally received nonverbally from these beings. She describes these inspired writings as being, in a sense, her art form. I've always felt particularly uplifted and empowered by a message from the Wild Violet Deva, excerpted here:

> You find in us a power and authority as great as that of the large trees, although we are the smallest flower you have contacted. Yes, this is because we are wild, well-established, free to roam, not dependent on the whims of man... You cannot cease wondering at the power of my voice. I have found my niche, I am where God means me to be, and therefore I am as powerful as any in the land. I AM power– I, the synonym for shyness! Nothing in this world or the next can shake those who follow their ordained pattern and do God's will unreservedly. Find and follow God's will for you, and your voice will be power.

In 1980, Leslie and I arrange to bring Dorothy Maclean to Fayetteville. She speaks to over two hundred people in the UARK Theater then leads a weekend workshop in which she teaches the participants attunement, and practices it with us as we intentionally connect with different energies of Nature including, memorably, The Spirit of the Ozarks bioregion.

Leslie and I subsequently have a number of stunning experiences with attunement. Here's one: some time after Dorothy visits us in 1980, we sit at the edge of a two acre field we've cleared for food growing in the hills near Kingston, Arkansas. We want to practice attunement and agree to tune in to "The Spirit of the Wind." We close our eyes and drift to a relatively quiet place inside ourselves. Once there, we briefly hold a clear intention to contact that aspect of Nature, then resume our immersion in silence. I reopen my eyes first. Standing a few feet from us is a ten foot tall whirlwind. Astonished, I whisper "Look!" to Leslie, who opens her eyes and joins me in amazed contemplation of this windy anomaly. It stays long enough to be well-witnessed, then whisks away.

This event is one of many we've had which I'd call "confirmatory experiences," in that they have dramatically reinforced our confidence in the responsiveness of natural forces to the resonance of clear, focused human awareness. As you might imagine, our immediate reaction to the whole incident is a giant "WOW!"

The Findhorn Community has made a huge positive difference in my life. While there, I began to sense the universe as utterly unified, yet distinctively unique at every point. Here are three poems I wrote while traveling in Scotland in 1969-70, very much under the influence of Findhorn's vision of the Spirit indwelling and sustaining all aspects of Nature:

The Isle of Iona

Iona is the passionate, ascetic
heart of Scotland, protected by its own
desolation; grave of kings set in the veins
of an icy sea.

The Tarot of Iona would include images
of its ancient abbey, with indwelling
devas, the white fringe of spray
ringing her shores, the cell of St. Columba,
the Christian lamb, the wind that speaks
this island's mind to each pilgrim
who passes here.

It was lambing season when I arrived on Iona
and secured a room at the Black's, in a shed perched
away from their farmhouse. Mr. Black was a horse-
sized man, one of generations of Iona farmers, with

great blue eyes the earth had informed with peace,
with his own birds flying through his thoughts,
and fingers that will be strong at death.

Mrs. Black was a shy mainlander he'd met thirty
years ago, she vacationing, she never really falling
into the rhythm of the sea-locked seasons here,
never quite accepting resident saints into her dreams.

In a stone-walled field
near the manse, at the sea's doorstep
two bent trees, fifty yards apart. Each evening there,
a flock of crows and one of sparrows would fly within
the strictures of that square, turning past each other
like a gust of stars, two motions of a single mind.

Iona seen through a glass darkly.
At night I would sit on rockpeak, under wind's hand,
under a pierce of stars, playing the penny whistle.
And never in day could I recall the melodies
that unwound, but my head felt like flame
and I felt visiting hints of Pan as
the music rose like Celtic incense
during the long night...

Those apparent "hints of Pan" reported in the above poem
could have been intuitions of an actual contact. It is also plausi-
ble that my experience may have arisen totally or in part from my
prior reading of a Findhorn pamphlet containing R. Ogilvie Crombie's narrative of his encounter with Pan on Iona in May, 1966. In
either case, what I discerned felt powerful and wild, and somewhat reminiscent of Kenneth Grahame's numinous description of
the approach of Pan in his book The Wind in the Willows:

This is the place of my song-dream, the place the music played to me," whispered the Rat, as if in a trance. "Here, in this holy place, here if anywhere, surely we shall find Him!"

Then suddenly the Mole felt a great Awe fall upon him, an awe that turned his muscles to water, bowed his head, and rooted his feet to the ground. It was no panic terror--indeed he felt wonderfully at peace and happy--but it was an awe that smote and held him and, without seeing, he knew it could only mean that some august Presence was very, very near... And still there was utter silence in the populous bird-haunted branches around them; and still the light grew and grew.

As children, R. Ogilvie Crombie and I both read the above passage and the magnificent description of Pan that follows it in Grahame's book, which may well have conditioned the ways in which both us perceived and personified the ubiquitous sacred intelligence known historically in the West as "Pan." You can find previously unpublished accounts of Ogilvie's meetings with Pan and other Nature beings in The Occult Diaries of R. Ogilvie Crombie, by Gordon Lindsay, edited by David Spangler.

Iona is steeped in deep peace, as is Mull, another of approximately one hundred and forty four Hebridean islands set off the West Coast of Scotland:

The Isle of Mull

Cloud and light clubs break over granite Mull.
    The plover lays her polished eggs
    in an open keep of sand and bone.
Waves roam down the earth's slow curve.
High tors of lark song spur the wind.
    The silence of the world mends here.

I sensed that the tranquility of Mull was like a balm on the wounds of our clamorous human world. Places like this must be preserved.

I also spent some time with a welcoming farm family living on Black Isle, a peninsula located to the west of the Moray Firth and Findhorn. This portrait of the mother of the family emerged shortly after my visit:

Morag Clouston

A poem about you, Morag Clouston,
    how you walked through the farmhouse
in morning hush after night snow,
    dusting the heirlooms and old oak.
Kitchen tableaux: of you dicing carrots,
    or reading as supper simmered,
or carrying in stew
    to your man and three boys
(them dressed in blue shirts,
    smiling and a little quiet
with one another in the candlelight).
    Then a simple thing, you turn about
in the kitchen to clatter dishes
    back into the cupboard, lamplight
across your back and soft spun hair.

A poem to picture you
    home in your hills,
spending hours in sun-dust
    on the back stairs with a green
congregation you watered and sang to.
    What words would be transparent,
shapely as a wineglass held out
    to you, weary woman, to pour
how you paused at the gate late one night
    in your forty-fifth winter,
the boys in bed, and took in

the night's whole glitter?
How the hoarfrost crackled all around
   as if it were being hammered,
and you thought,
   "I could dance like the children",
feeling light as a whisper
   before the lingering stars,
and how close to the skin,
   how awake was the young girl in you,
Morag Clouston.

Something dormant or dozing in us may suddenly wake as we pause under the stars, or while we minister to a "green congregation" of house plants. My sojourns at Findhorn have helped me understand how our day to day intimacies with Nature can facilitate such awakenings.

Stirring Up a Hornet's Nest of Wasps (1980)

Yes, wasps, nesting up under an eave of the six-sided cabin in northwest Arkansas where we live off and on from 1979–1981. Their papier-mâché-like home is way too close to ours for our comfort. Because I try my utmost not to kill insects, I decide to attune to "waspness," that is, the presiding energy template or deva of the species, and ask them to leave.

It's a hot summer afternoon. I'm trying to attune, but I fall into a woozy half-sleep beneath the wasps' abode. Next thing I know, the very Wasp of wasps--close to a foot in length!--flies down and lights on my right hand and impales me with its stinger. I sense I have to take this if I want real contact, and I do, so I keep my right hand still by force of will and endure significant pain. As this is happening, I tell the Wasp of wasps I want these wasps to leave their nest. Within the next day or two, they do. For good. And I'm left with an odd aftereffect: for years, each time I see a wasp I feel a faint iteration of the Big One's sting, sometimes in or around my right hand, but often most distinctly in the subtle crown of energy just above my head.

Some months later, we experience an infestation of fleas in our one-cat home. I attune to the deva of that species, and see a mental action-shot of fleas hopping out our front door. After that, the little guys never bug us again.

"The Spirit Likes to Make These Lights" (1980–1984)

First Magical Memories of Fatherhood

July 22, 1980:

We fast for a week
and pray, to purify.
There in the little cabin,
I feel the moment
our son's light arrives,
at the point
of his conception.

*

That memory moves me
back to Leslie's sixth or seventh
month of pregnancy.
We lie down
on our bed to drowse
and for about ten minutes
I experience her body
and Adam's own curled up
inside her, as vividly
as I feel mine.
The current of awareness
circles through us,
as us.

*

That memory-link reminds me
of the morning after
Adam's birth. The doctors
won't dare let him nurse
until he spends about nine hours
away from us, for fear
that he might contract the infection
Leslie's developed during her long labor.
We pine for him
in our hospital room,
many sterile rooms away
from where Adam lies
in his lonely incubator.
Resting in our room,
I find myself profoundly
merged with him,
attendant on his gentle
respiration and heartbeat.
All boundaries dissolve
as my élan flows out
to nurture our newborn.

*

Later on at home,
the window closed:
thin porcelain scrapings,
then whistles ghosted
out of silence:
joyous bird-songs swirl out
over Adam's crib.

*

About two years later,
I go to that same room
alone. In deep meditation,
my auric field expands
and begins a slow rotation
through our home.
As my extended consciousness
sweeps through Adam and Leslie
in an adjoining room,
Adam calls out, "Hi, Dad!"

*

Let's progress
in time now to a few months
after those strange rotations:
Going upstairs with Adam, age 3,
at 11 p.m., he pauses and says, "We should stop
if we see a light like a bubble. Some
are brown, some pink, white and silver
and red." A nebula of bright spirit lights
swarm and dance above us on the stairs.
I've often seen such lights, sometimes with others,
outdoors over herb and flower beds,
or in the woods by creeks, or in *inipi*
(sweat lodge) ceremonies, but rarely indoors,
or so brilliant. We watch.
"The Spirit likes to make these lights,"
I say, "they're part of its joy."
"Yeah," Adam replies. "Do you know
what they're called?"
"What name do YOU give them?"
I ask him. He says,
"They're called the 'brown leaf bubble.'
The Spirit can blow red and brown bubbles.
It can do that."

*

Our world has brimmed
with love and play
and real magic.
He is my son
and I have become
one of the loves
that overflows to him.
These sacred little tales
I offer to remind:
love lives us all.

"Ah...Buddha" (1982–1983)

Shortly after we purchase our first house in Fayetteville, several things happen there involving our son Adam. One night in 1982 a few weeks after we move in, I stand outside our back door next to him as he dozes in his stroller. He's not quite one and a half years old. As I look at Adam's peaceful sleeping face, I think of angels and buddhas, and at that moment he joins his hands together in a prayerful way, makes a perfect gassho (the Buddhist word for bowing respectfully to another with palms and fingers joined), then returns to motionless rest.

About eight months later, while sleeping next to Adam, Leslie awakens from a funny dream in which I offer her a worm to eat. Adam wakes as well, and says, "I like worms, Mom." Around this same time, I'm planning where to put up posters I've designed to publicize a workshop I'm going to offer. Adam, leaning against my knee, says "Posters" all of a sudden. I'm sure I haven't said the word out loud.

Many have noticed that infants and young children are open to subtle energies and communications. Leslie and I jot down the above and other similar events in Adam's baby book. The most important to me of these incidents transpires one winter evening in 1983 as Adam and I lie side by side in our back bedroom. He's almost two years old. He's asleep; I am half awake. I suddenly sense a malign presence float into the room from outside the house. It seems to hover near the foot of the bed. As this occurs, Adam lets go a long groan in his sleep: "Daddy...aahhrr." Not wanting to wake him, I begin to mentally repeat Guru Padmasambhava's potent mantra OM AH HUM VAJRA GURU PADME SIDDHI HUM, with nary a sound escaping my lips. As I do this, Adam says "Ah... Buddha" loudly and clearly in his sleep, and the malign feeling is immediately replaced by a beautiful feeling of liquid light.

Peace. We rest. I never forget this transformative moment, and often chant the mantra during the next eight years. When we invest mantras and other traditional spiritual practices with some measure of genuine faith and trust, they may help us tap into the power of our own wholeness. In 1991, I vow to Tibetan Buddhist teacher Sogyal Rinpoche to chant the Vajra Guru mantra every day for the rest of my life. And that has been a most rewarding practice.

Ghosts, Buster (1982–1983)

After we move into our house in Fayetteville, I receive other early intimations of spirit-activity around the place. I dream of a group of people dressed in nineteenth century clothing. They stand quietly together behind our house in the yard of an old farmstead that has been inhabited since before the Civil War. When I chant my Buddhist mantra for their liberation in the dream, a middle-aged-looking spokeswoman approaches me respectfully and says, "Sir, we're Christian ghosts." So I invoke Christ, and an enormous fountain of white light streams up and carries them heavenward to what I presume to be higher levels of awareness.

About a year later, our housemate Patti remarks on a face peeking at us around the edges of thresholds, at the peripheries of our visual fields. I too notice this same phenomenon, particularly when listening to Van Morrison's uplifting "Inarticulate Speech of the Heart" album while recklessly sawing away on an old violin as accompaniment. Perhaps that corrugated scraping on my violin has dragged the spirit down to earth in sheer consternation!

Anyway, until one hot summer night, neither Patti nor I see any more than that curious, furtive face. Now, I lie in bed next to Leslie. Restless, I decide to walk downstairs and grab a snack to settle myself down for sleep. As soon as I step into the hall, I see the floating smoky purple torso of an apparition lingering at the top of the stairs. I head right toward it, gathering my courage and centering my mind on the same liberating Vajra Guru mantra which I've inwardly intoned before when encountering what seemed to be disembodied entities.

Summoning up all the resolve I can in the seconds it takes to cross the hall, I walk right through the purple torso, chanting and offering the mantra to free this being from entrapment in an earthbound realm. I then continue on downstairs to enjoy my snack. A little later, I climb the phantom-free stairway to our bedroom and Leslie--half-awake and unaware of what has happened in the darkened hall--greets me with a puzzled, "What was that? It looked like a black moth, but it flew out through the screen." An open window frame with a securely closed screen to keep out insects is right behind the bed. Leslie can't figure how a moth could exit there, though she knows she's just seen some small black thing departing by that route. But I know what has left. We never see or sense that curious face peep around a threshold in our house again.

Who's There? (1982, 1990, 2000)

I'm meditating at the Transcendental Meditation Center in Fayetteville. Deep quietude. In my mind's ear, I hear two knocks. In a few seconds, two actual knocks sound out from a door far down the block. I hear the door swing open.

Over time, an interesting sort of theme emerges around doors opening: In 1990, the whole family visits Leslie's father and his second wife in Connecticut. They're extremely leery of extrasensory possibilities and claims. One day during our visit, we await two of Leslie's other relatives who are coming for lunch. They're running late, and we all wonder when they'll arrive. I hear an inner voice say that they'll come at one o'clock, and proclaim this boldly to Leslie's father and his wife. At exactly one, I get up from the table and go to the front door and open it. Leslie's relatives stand there, one of them with his arm raised and poised to knock. It seems like this synchronous scene's designed especially for Leslie's father and his wife as an assertion of the possibility of psi!

Around ten years later, I'm sitting in a family meeting, awaiting a cousin who has had to travel a long distance to attend. We've held off from plowing into the agenda, but after about forty minutes, we're getting antsy to begin. I'm suddenly impelled to rise, walk to the double doors, and fling them open. There's my cousin, his hand extended toward the door knob, surprised to be greeted before entering the meeting.

In neither of the above events was I conscious of hearing sounds outside the doors prior to opening them, although I may have been subliminally aware of normally inaudible footsteps. Again, I tend to see such synchronicities as little demonstrations meant to open doors in skeptical minds, more likely purposeful rather than simply being unconsciously registered or purely arbitrary events.

You'll find one more especially dramatic door-opening story when you get to the entries for 2011.

Therapeutic Telepathy (1983)

A woman I've never met comes for a few sessions of psychotherapy, and in the first reveals that a man has engaged her in a torrid affair. She offers no description of her suitor or seducer, just a bare confessional account delivered briefly with a mounting sense of distress. Suddenly two words surge up out of my mouth--her secret lover's name! The poor lady nearly jumps out of her skin. Thereafter, she appears uneasy whenever she sees me out in the community. I haven't meant to shock her, but the man in question is married with children, so perhaps my baffling blurt, which lifts the lid on this affair and helps startle her into discontinuing it, serves to avert further subterfuge and hurt.

Finding Rings (1983 and 2011)

My golden wedding band's been lost and found two times. First, at our old house, where it somehow falls off into the grass of the large yard. I can't find it myself, and after a month or so, I just give up the search. A short time later, after reading about unhealthy "geopathic earth zones" in Tompkin and Bird's book Secrets of the Soil, I ask the master dowser and healer Harold Mc-Coy to come over and check our home and land for any noxious subterranean influences.

Harold was a military intelligence officer for twenty-four years. He told me once that he'd dowsed and successfully found wells overseas during his years in the Armed Services. After retiring at the rank of Major, he served for a time as president of the American Society of Dowsers, then founded the Ozark Research Institute with his wife Gladys.

Now, Harold cruises our yard with his dowsing rods. First, he passes a cluster of bushes near our house, where a few years previously I had invited the local Nature spirits to hang out. I don't tell Harold of this prior invitation, but as he passes the bushes, he exclaims, "Oh, the Nature spirits love it right here. They're just sparkling in there."

Next Harold tells us that he's located several veins of underground water, one or two of which flow under our home and which may be less than optimal for our health, according to the findings of dowsers and others experienced with this rather esoteric field of healing lore. Harold "treats" the underground streams like an acupuncturist would a human patient, inserting long copper needles into two specific spots in the body of the earth close to our home. As he's strolling from one of these insertion points to the next, he suddenly exclaims, "What's this?" in surprise, and I watch his hand plunge down into the tall grass and grasp and pull up something that he's sensed rather than seen. Harold hasn't picked a flower; it's my lost, wandering ring!

The ring wears well on my left hand from that moment to a winter day in 2011. I've lost quite a bit of weight during a recent illness, and it fits so loosely on my finger that I inadvertently fling it off while tossing clumps of autumn-fallen leaves from off the path outside the front door of our current home. I search and search, to no avail. So I ask the Nature spirits of the area to help me, and envision them somehow returning the ring from wherever it lies hidden under dense ground cover to an easy-to-see place on the concrete pad directly fronting our front steps.

Nothing happens for about a week after this visualization/invitation for assistance. Then the gutter-screen replacement crew I've hired arrives to do their work, and the head guy on the crew walks through a plant-tangled part of the yard to the side of the concrete pad. He notices a swift golden blur, then hears a metallic "ping" and sees he's somehow kicked a ring out from under the thick ground cover while walking. There it lies, right on the spot where I'd recently envisioned it being magically returned! He rings the doorbell, ring in hand, and Leslie comes to the front door and receives the ring, and the story of its sudden reappearance.

She can hardly wait to show me, and when I come downstairs a few minutes later, she holds it in her closed fist, says, "I have a surprise for you," then reveals my twice-found ring and recounts how and where it was found. I tell her about my request for help a week earlier, and we marvel together, "Now what were the chances of that happening?"

Getting In Touch with Therapeutic Touch, Plus a Chuckle (1984 and 1993)

Pumpkin Hollow, New York: I attend a weeklong training in Therapeutic Touch, a system of energy-directed healing developed by professor of nursing Dolores Krieger and clairvoyant mystic Dora Van Gelder Kunz. During the week, we practice sensing and diagnosing felt irregularities in each others' energy fields, and directing healing to areas in need of it. Many times, we participants correctly diagnose existing physical imbalances without foreknowledge of them. After returning to Arkansas, I add Therapeutic Touch (T.T.) to my practice as a licensed massage therapist, and teach the technique to medical professionals and in public workshops.

A few years later, I begin to study hypnosis in order to enhance my skills as a licensed clinical social worker. I take many trainings with faculty of the Milton H. Erickson Foundation and the American Society for Clinical Hypnosis (the A.S.C.H.), which Dr. Erickson founded. I note the similarity between T.T. and the "mesmeric passes" famously practiced and taught by Anton Mesmer (1734-1815) to induce hypnotic trance. As one of the first master's degree members of the A.S.C.H., previously open only to people with Ph.D. and M.D. degrees, I associate with author and healer Eric D. Leskowitz, M.D. and other clinicians in the "Transpersonal Division" of that organization, and for two years serve as a faculty member, making presentations at annual scientific meetings.

In 1993, I make a presentation which involves teaching and demonstrating T.T., and discuss its similarities to mesmerism and modern clinical hypnosis. During the demonstration, I ask for a volunteer from the audience to come up and receive a full session of T.T..

The gentleman who volunteers sits quietly as I run my hands over his body, not making direct contact with him, but feeling his energy field for areas of irregular heat, denseness, or subtle roughness. There is only one area that seems different, a place at his mid back that is somehow uneven, less smooth to pass my hands over. It feels risky to me to announce this in front of the crowd of distinguished doctors, but I do, and am mightily relieved when my subject says that I've identified the one area of his body where he's been experiencing mild pain. After I direct healing energy to that area, he reports a diminution of the discomfort. It's a validating incident for me, and mind-opening for some members of the audience.

As a humorous addendum, I haven't always found such professional conferences to be as productive and inspiring as the one described above. The following song lyric illustrates some of the precipitous pitfalls of pursuing a continuing education in the mental health field:

Geoff Oelsner, LCSW's Dream*

While flying home on a plane going west,
I fell asleep for to take my rest.
I dreamed a dream fit for an anal analyst,
about my education as a psycho…therapist.

With half-dazed eyes I gazed to the room
where I'd just spent several endless afternoons
at a therapists' convention a-getting "CEU's"--
that's "continuing education" for my licensure renewal.

The place was an icy cold air-conditioned tomb--
your generic mirrored windowless hotel convention room,
where many a well-fed, well-paid, pompous, boring lecturer
spoke of many an aberration and bizarre, uncertain cure.

In such rooms I've learned hypnosis in a stuporous, deep
    trance;
studied Freud and Jung and Erickson, and cast an addled
    glance
at other famous therapists and their pet theories,
taught by their young pet devotees with goatees and degrees.

Now some of these were truly wise, quite kind and human,
    too,
but others were wired as Airedales and didn't have a clue.
Some played with a full deck, but the rest did surely not.
I wondered did they play at all? They looked quite lost in
    thought.

Others led encounter groups for emotional release.
They seemed to be resistant just to sit and shoot the breeze.
When on break I'd try to talk with them about things mun-
    dane but real,
like politics or sports, they'd ask [*this actually happened*],
    "Geoff…how does that make you feel?"

I dreamed we spoke of breakthroughs, instant insights by the
    score.
We plumbed to depths transpersonal, authentic to the core,
chakras open, roundly centered, quite correctly clinical--
the very model of a modern mental health professional.

By the end of this dream-afternoon, our exhausted heads
    were hung.
Into pitchers full of ice water we lolled our frozen tongues.
It seems that we had finally got our therapeutic fill…
a room of psycho…therapists full of intrapsychic swill.

While flying home on a plane going west,
I fell asleep in my Brooks Brothers vest.

I dreamed a dream fit for an anal analyst,
about my education as a psycho...therapist.

*Sung to the tune of the old English ballad, "Lord Franklin's La-
ment." Thanks and a tip o' the Oelsner hat to the immortal Bob
Dylan for inspiring me with his song "Bob Dylan's Dream" (from
his second LP, The Freewheelin' Bob Dylan, Columbia Records,
1963) which is set to the very same venerable melody.*

White Light, White Heat (1985)

I'm experimenting with long water and juice fasts. Around the
end of the second week of a cleansing fast, I'm present as Leslie
gives birth by cesarean section to our second child, Amy Claire.
We rest and blissfully bond together for several days in our hospital room before taking her home.

Many have noticed that the veil between this world and the
subtle realms is thinner at and after times of birth, as well as at
death. The English poet William Wordsworth worded this most
worthily in his great poem "Ode. Intimations of Immortality from
Recollections of Early Childhood" (1807) :

Our birth is but a sleep and a forgetting:
The Soul that rises with us, our life's Star,
Hath had elsewhere its setting,
And cometh from afar:
Not in entire forgetfulness,
And not in utter nakedness,
But trailing clouds of glory do we come
From God, who is our home:
Heaven lies about us in our infancy.

Almost as good is the little rhyme my grandmother taught me:

"Where do you come from, baby dear?
Out of the everywhere into the here."

91

We feel the sacredness that haloes Amy's birth as we relax "into the here" in the hospital. I'm in an altered state already from my long fast. The day after our daughter's arrival, I take an afternoon nap and find myself in a highly charged condition, keenly aware that I am free in this moment to surrender identification with ego and merge with "the everywhere," the transcendental Light. I opt for that choice, and after making a brief transitional passage through deeply-held psychophysical tensions, I disappear into sheer boundless white light for an indeterminate time. I then spontaneously "reappear," walking through part of the hospital in my astral body, radiant and heavy with blessing, before finally returning fully to my body and familiar human personality.

After a few minutes of absorbing the power and wonder of the mergence, I sit up and begin to tell Leslie what has just happened. She says, " You have a white light around your head. I've never seen that around anyone before." Evidently, I've come back from my sojourn beyond form "trailing clouds of glory" which are momentarily visible, at least to my generally down to earth partner.

"Don't Go Walking in Graveyards at Night Anymore" (1985)

I see her at a party for the Caribbean poet Derek Walcott. She's making all the soft, seductive moves that women do when they want to be taken home, not by me, but by the powerful brilliant poet who's just given a terrific reading on the University of Arkansas campus. Evidently, though, she's watched me watching her come-hither stuff, and has somehow found out who I am, because next thing I know, she's showed up as a first-time client. And it's clear she's set her cap for me. She's doing things--things I can and cannot see--to reel me in.

I'm a bit flattered by the sexual subtext but won't go anywhere remotely near the bait. As our session comes to an end, I tell her, apropos of nothing that's been said before, "Don't go walking in graveyards at night anymore." She's completely stunned to hear this, and admits she often takes dark walks among the dead.

Later, my clairvoyant spiritual friend Kenneth Cohen tells me that he's *seen* this young woman in a shamanistic context, and advises extreme caution: "Keep your distance from her; her soul has been possessed by the spirit of a black panther." I can't vouch for the literal truth of the panther part, but in retrospect Kenneth's predatory image makes sense.

"You're White Trash!" (1985)

I'm not proud of this one. I'm waiting at a stop light in Fayetteville, somewhat bleary-eyed and grouchy, on my way to work. In front of me in a funky banged-up pickup truck is a guy I rashly stereotype as a "redneck." My car windows are closed, and I don't recall his windows being open, either. I say under my breath, "White trash, white trash", and am utterly shocked as he instantly swivels around in his seat, looks daggers back at me, and says, "I ain't no white trash. *You're* white trash." I "hear" his powerful retort clearly though the busy intersection hum of idling engines and the stream of work-bound moving traffic. His words sear my inner ears, teaching me a necessary lesson.

Digging Under the Light (1986)

Jessieville, Arkansas: On one of thirteen trips to the Coleman Crystal Mine made in the early to late 1980's, I walk out one morning in the cool of the day, and see a light hovering over a particular patch of ground. I walk over to the light, take my trowel, dig directly under it to a depth of about two to three inches, and find the largest crystal cluster of that entire two day mining expedition.

Many luminous visual and energetic experiences unfold during these trips to the mines. The kids like camping in a remote spot at the back of the mines, so we often make a campfire there and sit around it after a day of digging and scanning the earth's surface for crystalline glints. Biding by the fire, I witness hours of pellucid, intricate visions of crystals, including seams of crystal deposits way under the earth. My visions are accompanied by a sense of complete oneness with these seams. It's an earth-initiation of some sort which involves my mind merging with a highly vibratory, precisely structured nonhuman intelligence.

At one point, I travel in vision to the center of a crystal hill somewhere in the Ouachita Mountain region and am privy to a council of vast crystal beings. At another point, I experience crystals I've found, or purchased at the mine's store, as being set inside different areas of my body, and very tangibly at that. On waking and scrunching out of my pup tent one morning, I find a huge single crystal point right at the entrance of my tent. I'm camping alone in an unpopulated spot, and that big beauty was definitely not there the night before when I crawled into my tent.

It's a time when Mother Earth begins to speak to me more clearly, and I begin to listen more deeply to what She's saying. It all starts for me at the Coleman Crystal Mine, but it doesn't end there. My spiritually gifted friend Kenneth Cohen has studied with advanced teachers from many traditions about the therapeutic applications of crystals, and a seemingly endless list of other natural modalities. (I highly recommend his book Honoring the Medicine: The Essential Guide to Native American Healing.) Kenneth teaches me more about crystal lore, including some of the ways they've been used by both Cherokee tribal people and Chinese Taoists for healing.

In the aforementioned book, Voices of Our Ancestors: Cherokee Teachings from the Wisdom Fire, the Ven. Dhyani Ywahoo, a member of the traditional Etowah Band of the Eastern Tsalagi (Cherokee) Nation, has written about Cherokee crystal teachings, and much more about her people's approaches to establishing harmonious relations with the earth and within ourselves. Her depth of understanding as the twenty-seventh generational holder of this ancestral wisdom makes her book a tremendous resource for earth-healing. Dhyani Ywahoo is also a teacher of Vajrayana Buddhism, having been recognized and empowered by H.H. Chetsang Rinpoche, the head of the Drikung Kagyu order, and other Tibetan Buddhist teachers. She has established Sunray Peace Village and the Vajra Dakini Nunnery in Vermont for those who wish to learn and practice Cherokee and Vajrayana teachings.

As I travel about, I begin a regular practice of leaving crystals and other rocks I've found as love-offerings to the land and the spirits of the land. I discover that singing songs and picking up trash both tend to build a stronger connection with spirits in the places I'm visiting. A little later, I amplify on these practices by obtaining Tibetan "Earth Treasure Vases," ceremonially made and blessed under the direction of Lama Kunga Thartse of the Ewam Choden Tibetan Center in California. I bury them in places around our town and areas where environmental harmony has been badly disrupted, such as near the Arkansas Nuclear One Units 1 and 2 power plants in Russellville, Arkansas.

Over the past twenty years, a woman I know named Cynthia Jurs has buried twenty-three or more of these ritual Earth Treasure Vases in locations around the planet. A Vajrayana Buddhist form of white magic, they are made with a meditative intention to bless and heal the earth. They contain crystals and scores of other sacred substances and medicines. A number of Tibetan Buddhist teachers are creating, distributing, and burying these vases. You can read more about their collective blessing-work at Cynthia Jurs' website, www.earthtreasurevase.org.

What's Shakin'? (1987)

On a number of nights, I come to bed last. It's our gigantic Family Bed, with Mommy, Daddy, Adam, and Amy all aboard. On some of these late nights, when I finally hit the hay, I lie awake awhile before sleep and notice that the massive old futon bed's vibrating. I can't figure this out--the only rational explanation is a big street cleaner or some other heavy machinery nearby shaking our house, and with it the bed. But no mechanical sounds resound.

After a few nights of this, I trace the mysterious shaking back to its source: Leslie's uterus! I can feel a strong vibration starting there, and emanating outward evenly to the whole bed. The family sleeps right through it. I finally bring this up to Leslie, and am surprised to learn that she's noticed the bed vibrating, too. I say, "Leslie, we'd better really watch our birth control. It feels to me like there's a soul wanting to come in here."

Not absolutely knowing this is so, we take a cautious course, adding extra safety precautions. But Leslie gets pregnant anyway. The day the test comes back positive, we two (now three) sit outside in the front yard and have a thorough discussion about the pluses and the minuses of bringing a third child into the world. We want this baby to be totally wanted, so we begin to talk seriously, in order to air and hopefully to clear any resistance (mainly mine) to having a third child. Right after we have voiced all of our negative concerns, Leslie suddenly stands up, rushes upstairs to the bathroom, and effortlessly miscarries.

We wonder if the soul that vibrated us and later was physically conceived against all contraceptive odds has now responded to our reservations by voluntarily departing. We ache and grieve and then move on. We never feel the Family Bed vibrate that way again.

Rattlesnake Man (1987)

At the Walnut Valley Bluegrass Festival in Winfield, Kansas: there are many crafts booths set up, and under the main stage bleachers is one devoted entirely to rattlesnake skin belts, hat bands, and other paraphernalia, including some detached dried rattles. The tall, wiry, tight-wound looking man who mans the booth is all decked out in rattlesnake skin cowboy boots, an elaborate hand-tooled belt, and a wide hat band on his black Stetson. He smells so strongly of nicotine, he somehow seems to me to be composed of it.

Every time I get within fifty feet or so away from him or his booth, I wince from the awful toxic sensation of rattlesnake venom, a felt sense of raw snake energy appropriated and cut and stitched into various forms of sartorial machismo. The feeling is so toxic that I soon begin to give that booth a mighty wide berth as I make my way through the long room. No way I want to get anywhere close to that old rattlesnake man's bad medicine.

Fragrance Meets Me (1988)

Fayetteville: I walk into our house with a brand new, just-published copy of the book on natural radioprotective substances I've been researching and writing with Steven Schechter and other collaborators for over seven years. Now finally I have my copy in hand. From the front door to the stairs is only a few steps. As I begin to climb the stairs, I'm inundated with a delicate and beautiful fragrance. The house is empty; no one's home except for me. The fragrance follows me up the stairs, then disappears, never to return. My sense at the time is one of being greeted by a celebratory sign that conveys a feeling of "Job well done!" It's all very mysterious in a most joyous way; a kind of nod of appreciation from that dimension where the impetus for my involvement in the book originated.

Office Visit (1988)

Near Jemez Springs, New Mexico, on a camping trip with my friend David. We've pitched our tent in a lush little valley below a beautiful, remote hot springs. Tired from travel, I lie down to rest for awhile, and find myself circulating through the local environment as formless pure awareness, in an elliptical clockwise pattern perhaps an eighth of a mile long. I am at one with the natural features, yet also moving around and in some cases through them. I recall some of the wonderful rock formations there as clearly as I do my own bodily sensations.

As this subtle circulation continues, I hear the voice and feel the unquestioned presence of the great deceased Indian saint Neem Karoli Baba (c.1902-1973). The words I hear him say, "You're in my office," don't make a lot of rational sense to me, but then of course this is not a "rational" experience. Later I tell my friend S. D. about this experience. A longtime devotee of Neem Karoli Baba who had been with him in India, S.D. exclaims, "Neem Karoli Baba had a sort of inner sanctum at the back of his ashram that he called his 'office.' He'd meet with people there at times in private."

I'm surprised, but not totally flabbergasted, surmising Neem Karoli Baba's time-and-space-transcending capacities from an earlier firsthand experience. In 1981, as I nap in our little rental house on Watson Street in Fayetteville, Neem Karoli Baba appears to me in a dream, lifts me aloft, and carries me over the Himalayas. It's an overwhelmingly beautiful flight, and the first time I can recall having the impression of traveling through time as well as space.

It is quite possible that I dreamed of Neem Karoli Baba as a *signifier* of that in me which is wise, supportive, powerful, and transcendent of time and space. I have had visions and dreams about a variety of spiritual figures, both contemporary and historical, from most religious and some indigenous shamanic traditions. I don't immediately leap to assume that they all involve actual encounters. However, Neem Karoli Baba (like Sri Ramana Maharshi, Shirdi Sai Baba, Sri Anandamayi Ma, and other great recent Hindu spiritual realizers) has appeared to people all over the world at times of urgent need, in response to prayers, or even unbidden to some individuals without prior knowledge of his existence.

There are many examples of this phenomena of living and departed saints guiding, guarding, rescuing, healing, and blessing in Christian, Islamic, and other religious traditions. Following a visit to a small cave on Mt. Subasio in Italy where St. Francis used to contemplate, I wrote a poem about a lucid dream in which such an encounter seemed feasible:

Dream in Assisi

Sleeping in the Citadella Christiana
in Assisi, I dream I'm sitting
beyond the town walls under a fig tree.
Two rabbits approach me in the cover
of tall grass, glassy-eyed with a strange trust.
I know this is a dream, when the rabbits
vanish and are replaced by two
great snuffling wolves, which come
to my hand as if it is magnetic
here in a round meadow at the foot
of Mt. Subasio. Clouds wheel above,
then in the place of wolves
I see a herd of restive cattle.
I have to laugh, wondering what
the next vision could possibly be,
when a cloak of wind enwraps me
and leaves me at the crest of Mt. Subasio
staring straight into the eyes
of a slight and flaming man.
We stand there long enough
to recognize each other.

But there's a little more to relate about Neem Karoli Baba: Around 1998, I'm driving my car on a bridge over the White River near Goshen, Arkansas, when I suddenly sing out his name like a summoning call. Instantly thereafter, one of my tires explodes.

The speeding car wavers toward the left lane, but I make it across the bridge safely, avoiding collision or mishap. I feel I've been protected by Baba, whom I think of as a friend of the family to this very day.

Ram Das' (Richard Alpert's) books <u>Miracle of Love: Stories about Neem Karoli Baba</u> and the more recent <u>Be Love Now</u> contain my favorite anecdotes and biographical passages about his guru. I write this in clear view of a photo of the old holy man standing with three Himalayan village boys, under which is written a quote from him which I love: "The best form in which to worship God is every form."

Looking Back

Travel is wonderful, yet it's a blessing to be settled for some time in a place that you love, and we received that blessing during this period as our children grew up in a little wood heated home with a ten mile view to the west. The Nature oriented stories in this chapter are rounded out by tales and poems devoted to the tender changes fatherhood visited upon my heart, and our home here in these sheltering valleys and hills.

The ancient Ozark bioregion where we've lived since 1979 is a plateau region of climax oak forests and groves which is said to be older than the Rockies, the Appalachians, and the Himalayas combined. To live here is to feel cradled in a vast wooded expanse. The earth scrolls out like ancient suede, if seen from a bird's eye view on a sunny afternoon, when the leaves are down and brown. Native Americans lived here in bluff shelters and caves starting about 7500 years ago. Traces of their passage still remain.

As I came to know and love the land here more and more, it spoke to me in many tongues: in visions, in songs that arrived on the wind and in my dreams, in heart-shaped stones and archaic artifacts. As my relationship with the Ozarks developed, so did my sense of connection with the whole earth. I've tried to protect and advocate for this ecological niche, working to do so in grassroots alliances with many of the progressive friends we've made here over the past thirty-plus years, and in cooperative communion with the devas and Nature spirits of the area.

When I consider this phase in my life, I think of the phrase "the power of." It was about understanding and experiencing more fully the power of prayer to heal and help people in need; the power that is innate in times of transition like conception, birth, and death; the power of spiritual practices like meditation and mantra; the miraculous power of attunement to connect with all forms of life; the power of intuition when it is focused for the sake of pure research or in service to others; the powers of the earth itself, including the mineral kingdom; and most of all, the power of love. The stories in this chapter have largely dwelt upon my education in the harmonious, shared uses of such powers. I mean for them to evoke an empowering mindset--a heartset really--in readers; to summon up a sort of spiritual "Yes, we can!" attitude.

VI. Midlife Harvest

Untitled Sketch by Robert Sudlow

Talismans of Belonging and Love
(1989 and 1999)

It's my fortieth birthday and melancholy is upon me, as I stroll mindfully through the steep creek valley carved out below the place where our friend Joy Fox has built a serene retreat center called Wattle Hollow. The day is clear and my beloved walks near me as clouds tell their ever morphing parables. My eye-beams skim the rounded stones I stroll over like fingertips lightly shifting rosary beads.

I'm here, but I'm simultaneously submerged in choppy emotional waters. My attention is clogged with a question: Why haven't I grown more, done more, by forty? It's a brief preview for a full length film entitled "Geoff's Midlife Crisis." In the midst of all this external beauty and interior brooding, I hear a clear voice say, "You're about to receive a gift from Nature".

I keep threading my way up the creek bed from boulder to sun-warmed boulder for half a minute or more, then see what I take to be a white leaf. This leaf is underwater, fluttering back and forth in the current which rushes over it. Its rhythmic movement catches my eyes, and calls my right hand. I reach into the chill current, wrist to forearm deep, and receive a perfect white arrowhead.

The arrowhead is the only one Joy Fox has ever heard of being found or has herself found at this creek site. It intimates to me that I belong to the natural order, the Sacred manifest as Nature. There's a mysterious backstory to this event: years before, I traded sessions with another psychotherapist who practiced clinical hypnosis like I have for many years. He put me in a deep trance, and told me the story of an Indian brave who found a white arrowhead in a stream. That hypnotic induction was remarkably true-to-life and memorable--my finding of the arrowhead in a dreamlike state of mind, its appearance as a white light, the satisfaction of having it in hand--and it turned out to be prophetic.

Now a leap in time, and it's my fiftieth birthday. Happier, more upbeat than at forty, I'm standing near the creek at Wilson Park in Fayetteville, wondering if I might receive a birthday gift from Nature. I haven't found another arrowhead since turning forty. It's slightly embarrassing to share this next bit, but I suddenly blurt the words, "I'm a magic man!" Immediately after saying that, I spy a large unbroken atl atl point of grayish flint a pace away, a spearhead used for fishing or to hunt four-leggeds who drink and fish from this stream. It nestles into my hand, and I am blessed yet again with a talisman of belonging and Nature's conductive love.

(An expert associated with the University of Arkansas has confirmed both the arrowhead and the atl atl point as authentic.)

"Listen, Listen, Listen" (1990)

Leslie and I sit upstairs in our house in Fayetteville, discussing her departed paternal grandmother, Pauline Berman. We then meditate silently, with an intention to bless Pauline, wherever she may be. The song "Listen, Listen, Listen to My Heart's Song," springs up in my heart as I sit next to Leslie. It's for Pauline. Thinking Leslie will appreciate it, I begin to sing it out loud as she comes out of her meditation. Leslie tells me she has just been singing that song in her mind, as a prayer for Pauline. It's one we haven't sung for years.

I Lie Down and Fly Up (1990)

I've driven my van to New Mexico, and finally stop late at night by the highway somewhere southeast of Santa Fe, unable to stay awake any longer. I leave an offering for local spirits, then get back in the van and lie down. Soon, asleep and in a lucid state, I lift out of my weary body, pretzel-snap my astral double's legs into full lotus posture, and begin one of the longest, most visually detailed and awesome spirit flights of my life. I hover over miles and miles of moon-mottled rolling bushy arid land, flying several hundred feet below splotches of cloud. I estimate a seventy mile trajectory. The next day, I drive northwest over the territory where I've just projected, and though I've never driven on this stretch of road before, I find the landscape to be very much the same as it appeared in my awakened dream.

Lilacs à Deux (1991)

My office at 1 W. Mountain Street: There's one small window, never opened. I sit with a client who's here for clinical hypnosis, gradually opening his mind as the trance induction proceeds. I've asked him questions prior to beginning the induction, and learned that lilac is a scent he's always loved. So I mention lilac flowers during the induction, and my little office room is filled with lilac fragrance, which we both distinctly smell, despite that closed-up window. Folie à deux? A shared unconscious mutual consenus to scent in the absence of actual lilacs? We rest in the delicate smell. The lilac fragance eclipses all my other memories of that session.

Waves of White Light (1992)

Edwardsville, Illinois: I'm sitting in an all night Native American Church ceremony, and have closed my eyes to pray. I'm suddenly aware of waves of white light rippling across the room and breaking on the shore of my body. I open my eyes and find that the Roadman who leads this ceremony has produced a huge eagle feather, and is fanning the air in my direction from across the room, with the intention of cleansing and blessing.

What the Raven Gave Us (1993 and 1998)

Tesuque Pueblo

A Song for Amy Claire Oelsner

Oh the vastness of the turquoise that day in New Mexico
when we sat in the sun with the raven at Tesuque Pueblo.

In the ruins of the Old Ones,
we picked up pottery clay,
pieces of a once-joined jigsaw puzzle that Time
had swept away.

I brushed off the dust from a jagged shard
I'd wanted for my own, when I heard with a shock
a thought from the rock, saying,

"This is still our home."

So I put the piece down on its own home ground
and we scrambled on up the scree,
and I swore I'd never take a thing away
unless it was given to me.

Oh the vastness of the turquoise that day in New Mexico
when we sat in the sun with the raven at Tesuque Pueblo.

Los Alamos lies behind these hills,
the nuclear city
where they built the bomb called "the Gourd of Ashes"
in a Hopi prophecy.

But here in the eye of the afternoon sky,
we sit on the peaceable stone
on the rim of a cliff where the breezes lift,
and we don't feel quite alone.

Because the sun seeps into the cracks in the rocks
and the long bones of our limbs,
and the long river runs through the cottonwood trees
far below in the shivering wind.

Oh the vastness of the turquoise today in New Mexico
as we sit on the lip of an ancient cliff at Tesuque Pueblo.

A raven lofts just over our heads
and she circles us once with a call,
then she drifts with the breeze past the mesquite trees
that jut from the split cliff wall.

Well, we sit up straight and meditate

105

as that raven glides by on the wind,
then she spirals five feet over us
and calls to us again.

The third time she swoops over us,
soft wing-beats brush our heads,
then she lands on a rock about ten feet off
and stands there on a ledge.

Oh the vastness of the turquoise mind of the sky in
    New Mexico
as we sit in the sun with the raven at Tesuque Pueblo.

And under the sun, I feel we're seen
and known by the Ancient Ones,
and the raven's a sacred go-between
in this place of sentient stones.

In a timeless tide, we sit and bide
and the pieces all fit in a whole,
and we join our minds with the turquoise sky
circling us like a pottery bowl.

Oh I don't care if I'm nowhere
and the ages break my bowl.
I'll stay with you and the raven
where our pieces all are whole.
No I don't care if I'm nowhere
and the ages break my bowl.
I'll stay with you and the raven
where our pieces all are whole.

Then...the moment passed and the raven
flapped her wings and she flew away,

and there on the brink we heard a clink
and we saw something rock and sway.

Where that bird had stood was a pottery shard
and it moved though the wind was low.
I picked it up and felt a shock
at this gift from the great Unknown.

Oh the vastness of the turquoise that day in New Mexico
when we sat in the sun with the Ancient Ones at Tesuque
    Pueblo.

Five years later in Arkansas,
a girl holds the shard in her hand
and receives the power from that timeless hour
when the raven came to land.

As she opens to the living Spirit
in the summer of her thirteenth year,
her mother and I are swept by the tide
of what comes alive in her.

Then she goes to her room and writes a poem
that she reads to us that day,
and her mother and I both begin to cry
at the words we hear her say:

*

[*Here, with her permission, is Amy's poem*]:

"The earth is good all in all
People will learn people will fall
Everyone wants to be loved
The sea will love them

The wind and the mountains
The world will be, can be
Pure sweet love
The universe
Existence of all beings
Everything
Is a bright
Flow of
Lovely energy
With all the small
Amazing details at every
Corner and bend
I am you
You are me
If you're afraid of being
Different then don't make
Labels
We're creating our own worst
Fears
But we could and we will
I hope
All be the same wonderful energy
Of compassion inside and out"

*

So I don't care if I'm nowhere
and the ages break my bowl.
I'll stay with you and the raven
where our pieces all are whole.
No I don't care if I'm nowhere
and the ages break my bowl.
I'll stay with you and the raven
where our pieces all are whole.

His Holiness Chetsang's Blessing (1994)

Spring of 1994, a time of high stress. My hair's falling out; my need for physical and spiritual renewal is acute. I drive to the Tampa-Clearwater, Florida area to attend a five day teaching with the co-leader of the Tibetan Drikung Kagyu order of Buddhism, His Holiness Chetsang Rinpoche. He turns out to be my age, chronologically at least. In other ways he's rather more mature! I end up chauffeuring him and his small entourage of monks. Along the furious five and six lane highways we go racing. I'm nervous at first, then gradually more relaxed to be with these good-natured, red and maroon-robed passengers.

Later, after receiving formal teachings from him, I'm granted a private interview with H.H. Chetsang, and request his blessing. He produces a venerable looking metal box, peaked like a little portable temple, with unseen sacred objects inside. He places the box atop my head, holds it there and whispers prayers, and ever since that moment until now, the Inner Light's been brighter; the veil less dense between me and Essence.

Guided Home (1996)

As our children get older and we all require more personal space, our house on Vandeventer Street becomes too small. We begin to search for a new place, visiting perhaps ten or fifteen homes without being able to completely agree on any one of them. Then, I dream that an invisible guide is flying before me up a winding street. The guide and I arrive inside a house with large windows, through which I can see a patio. Though I don't recall additional details, I remember the way the street twists and turns as I fly uphill above it. This dream comes twice.

When we finally visit our current home for the first time, I'm struck by the way the street snakes around as it leads up to a house on a partially wooded lot. I feel that I've been up this road before, but not in a car! Large living room windows span most of a wall, facing a patio and a thickly wooded hill. This is one of about a dozen incidents which have built my trust in helpful, ethereal guides. Many people see distinct images of their guides. I generally do not, but occasionally can feel a benevolent presence directing and assisting me as I go about my waking or sleeping life. This sense of presence is often accompanied by goose bumps, or an enlivening of the subtle center above my head.

After we move into our new home, I sense a distressed quality about the hilly neighborhood. It feels like the land's been insensitively pushed around--bullied--and in fact it has: most lots have had to be graded by bulldozers before construction of the homes on them could commence. The majority of our new neighbors don't seem to spend much time enjoying or caring for their yards. It's rare to hear the voices of children at play. The area feels somewhat forsaken. Over several years, I pray, make offerings, bury an Earth Treasure Vase, meditate outdoors, get to know and appreciate the trees, and ask a friend who is a Native American Pipeholder to conduct a Sacred Pipe ceremony on behalf of our land. We start gardens, and generally love the place up. With time, the lot we live on begins to feel better to me. Gradually, the land responds to our love.

My Father's Prescient Prophecy (1996–1997)

We've celebrated Christmas at my parents' home in Shawnee Mission, Kansas, and now as I follow Leslie and our two children out the door, my father bids a disconcerting last goodbye to me: "Goodbye, Geoff. You know, I might die and you'll get all I have." I'm utterly surprised. Dad's in good health as far as any of us know. I turn around, re-enter the house and put my arms around him, saying, "Dad, I hope it will be a long time before that happens. I love you." Then we leave. But I can't shake the shaky feeling that I get from Dad's last words.

This turns out to be the final time I ever see my father, Geoffrey A. Oelsner, Sr., in the flesh. He dies of an abrupt heart attack just after finishing dinner with my mother in Phoenix, Arizona in March of 1997. In retrospect, I recall how he took me to see his lawyer and good family friend during that same Christmas visit, to better my understanding of some complexities of his estate. Did Dad have some presentiment of his passing? If so, he never discussed it with my mother.

I share this poem at his funeral:

Eulogy For My Father,
Geoffrey A. Oelsner, Sr. (1925–1997)

"We've been so blessed," Dad said to me
increasingly in his last years of life.
My father's voice brimmed up from some deep,
sweet place in himself that never took
a good for granted.

One blue Ozark morning a few months after
he'd retired, I asked him how it felt
to shift from working 6 A.M. to 6 P.M.
most weeks for forty years,
to his new sudden leisure.

He seemed to search that gracious place
inside himself for words, then said,
"It's hard to describe this, Geoff,
but since retiring I'm like a man floating
on his back out on the ocean.

"I can feel each wave beneath me, and I'm just
relaxing back and enjoying every moment."
He knew how to ride the tides, to rest within
the midst of motion, throughout a life
so full of gentle goodness:
the foremost goodness of my mother's love
for him, and his for her, forever;
the fun and satisfaction of dear lifelong friends;
the excellence of work and selfless service done
and then let go; a perfect serve hit cross the net
in slanting light!

And now...no final words well up in me
that might express my love for you,
except the ones you spoke to me:
We've been so blessed by you, Dad.
Geoff, we've been so blessed.

Yes, that prescient moment at my parents' door was the last time Dad and I met in the flesh, but quite possibly *not* the final time we ever got together. That's a cherished story for another occasion.

How the Hell Did I Do That? (1998 and 2011)

I attend an introductory week at the Monroe Institute in Virginia, a training facility for individuals who want to cultivate out-of-body and other paranormal abilities. Our group of approximately thirty participants is introduced to Joseph McMoneagle, for nineteen years the senior and most frequently accurate remote viewer in our government's classified "Project Star Gate" remote viewing intelligence gathering program.

Mr. McMoneagle speaks for awhile about himself and his incredible intuitive capacities. He describes the Star Gate program, and then invites us all to join in a remote viewing experiment ourselves. We're given six numbers as coordinates for a "target" we are to remote view, three for latitude and three for longitude. I sink into a quiet state and suddenly clearly "see" a huge cylindrical roughly grooved stone outcropping. We're given six more coordinates, and this time I seem to be but inches from a shining, smooth metallic surface which rises from a concrete base far up into the sky.

To my surprise, of the thirty folks who try this little experiment, a woman from Italy and I describe most exactly what the two targets turn out to be: the Devil's Tower in Wyoming and the St. Louis Arch. This gets my attention! I'm curious just how this kind of precision can be possible, and how such capacities might be applied to enhance scientific research.

Joseph McMoneagle has written four books about his remote viewing experiences, including the revealing <u>Remote Viewing Secrets: A Handbook</u> (2000) and <u>Star Gate Chronicles: Memoirs of a Psychic Spy</u> (2002). A partial curriculum vitae about him reads:

> During his career, Mr. McMoneagle has provided professional intelligence and creative/innovative informational support to the Central Intelligence Agency (CIA), Defense Intelligence Agency (DIA), National Security Agency (NSA), Drug Enforcement Agency (DEA), Secret Service (SS), Federal Bureau of Investigation (FBI), United States Customs (USC), the National Security Council (NSC), most major commands within the Department of Defense (DoD), and hundreds of other individuals, companies, and corporations. He is the only person who has successfully demonstrated his ability as a remote viewer more than one hundred times, live, double-blind, and under strict scientific control while on-camera for national networks and labs in six countries (including National Geographic, Discovery Channel, the BBC, ABC, CBS, NBC, Channel 4 England, and Nippon and Ashai TV in Japan).

Experienced as a researcher, Mr. McMoneagle has designed, conducted, and published the results of a number of remote viewing studies. His vitae continues:

> As a consultant to SRI-International and Science Applications International Corporation, Inc. from 1984 through 1995, he participated in protocol design, statistical information collection, R&D evaluations, as well as thousands of remote viewing trials in support of both experimental research as well as active intelligence operations for what is now known as Project STAR GATE. He is well versed with developmental theory, methods of application, and current training technologies for remote viewing, as currently applied under strict laboratory controls and oversight.

> He is a full time Research Associate with The Laboratories for Fundamental Research, Cognitive Sciences Laboratory, Palo Alto, California, where he has provided consulting support to research and development specifically within remote viewing for 25+ years.

This gentleman and his remote viewing peers in the Star Gate program worked under rigorously controlled conditions and protocols, often providing accurate or partially accurate and still useful answers to very specific, difficult questions which they were not shown! They were merely given geographic coordinates, or at times no prior information at all. In other words, they were intuitively gifted to the point that they gleaned some *questions* correctly, as well as their answers. Scientists who have collaborated with and observed Mr. McMoneagle attest to his Zenlike, pinpoint accuracy in Elizabeth Lloyd Mayer's book, <u>Extraordinary Knowing</u>. I'm not sure I'd find it easy to believe their assertions myself, but for my own experience at the Monroe Institute.

My encounter with Joseph McMoneagle proves providential later, in 2011, when I initiate the Psi-Sci (Psychics and Scientists) Alliance project to link scientists working in the field of climate change mitigation with psychics who have a demonstrable track record of success. I recontact Joseph, remind him of our brief meeting at the Monroe Institute, and am thrilled when he is willing to contract with me to work with a highly respected researcher I have met who is open-minded enough to engage in this unorthodox collaboration.

The aims of the Psi-Sci Alliance project are to advance research into productive approaches to the climate crisis, and more generally to help deconstruct unproductive barriers between science and the principled use of intuition. To these ends, the project seeks scientists, engineers, and inventors who are working on ways to ameliorate climate change, to team up with gifted intuitives who have provided accurate information to medical professionals, scientific researchers, and law enforcement and government intelligence agencies. The Monroe Institute, the Institute of Noetic Sciences (IONS), and the International Society for the Study of Subtle Energies and Energy Medicine (ISSSEEM) have all helped to publicize this Psi-Sci Alliance initiative.

There's a postscript to the above account; an incident of blessing and synchronicity involving a related climate awareness project: Also in 2010, I fly west to attend teachings by the Tibetan master H. H. Chetsang Rinpoche. My journey has multiple purposes--the very next day after receiving his teachings I'll be meeting with another researcher into possible approaches to mitigating climate change. So when the time comes for my private interview with the Rinpoche, I ask him to bless my work on behalf of the earth.

The next day, I'm a bit overwhelmed by a full schedule of meetings, both with the researcher, and with a cryologist (cryology being the scientific study of snow and ice, essential to the accurate observation of planetary climate change). I want to connect with yet another person during this short period of travel, a major climate change activist whom I'd previously met and corresponded with, but I'm just not sure that I'll have the time. I wander into a natural foods market to catch a quick lunch and, there he is, coming down an aisle near me!

We find a time to meet in the mid-afternoon, and when we do, he introduces me to a friend who is a seasoned documentary film maker. I've been wanting to get a two-pronged project off the ground. It doesn't take us long to find out that we've been thinking about more or less the same kind of project: the combination of a full-length documentary film and/or a number of shorter films featuring interviews with top climate scientists, which would then be linked with a website where all of the most current information on climate change will be posted.

About a year since that first meeting, my two friends have the film and a much more comprehensive network of websites than we had initially envisioned under production. They have graciously solicited my input, and have kept me informed about the progress of both projects.

Perhaps that fortuitous meeting in the market eventuated from the blessings of H.H. Chetsang Rinpoche. If we're willing to de-compartmentalize our highly specialized approach to research and development, we can engender fruitful collaborations between people from improbably different backgrounds. Spiritual masters, sages, indigenous shamans, medicine persons, and psychically gifted individuals can bless and augment the work of scientists, engineers, and inventors on behalf of Gaia. In this way, we may arrive at new paradigms and perspectives that will allow us to deal more effectively with urgent environmental issues. We must marshal *all* our intellectual and intuitive capacities to address the now-immediate survival challenges posed by accelerating climate change. We can do this. We can recognize and exercise our power to be activists for the earth.

Shocked by the Lama (1998)

Lake Canandaigua, New York: It's my second year at a summer retreat led by Vajrayana Buddhist teacher Lama Surya Das, and I've become his massage therapist. After one of the first massages I give Lama Surya, I return to my room downstairs and lie in bed thinking back on the experience of working on him. I unmindfully project my thoughts in his direction upstairs, through the ceiling, as it were. Having been so recently immersed in giving the massage, I retain a strong felt sense of his immense presence, so my thoughts seem to wing to him…almost. They're met with a mighty electrical barrier, which stops them very much like a bug zapper would an intrusive fly. It's an overwhelming, immediate sensation which chastens me and leaves me quite cautious about making any further unintentional mental excursions into his space, which seems to be surrounded with some kind of energetic electric fence, a potentially wrathful protective barrier.

Paranormal Electronics (1999)

We'd lived with Patti, a psychically sensitive young woman, in 1982–1983. Then for years, we'd hear from her occasionally, after she married and began a business selling medicinal herbs in Oregon. One day, a mutual friend gets in touch with us to let us know that Patti has died. A day or so after that, I get in my car, start it, and discover that the radio is on. I never leave the radio, lights, or AC on when I turn off the ignition, so this gets my attention. I resolve to be extra careful to check that the radio is turned off each time I leave my car, but within the next day the same thing happens again twice, and I catch an astral whiff of playful, sleeve-tugging mischief .

It seems possible that Patti has attempted to communicate her presence in a fashion that's often been experienced by others after the deaths of family or friends. Parapsychologists are familiar with the frequently reported phenomena of electric lights, telephones, tape recorders, and other electrical devices apparently being used by recently departed souls to communicate with friends and kin in this world. For more information on a thought-provoking aspect of this subject, a good starting-point is the research of Konstantins Raudive, a Latvian scientist, psychologist (he was a student of Carl Jung), and parapsychologist.

Raudive's book <u>Breakthrough</u>, about capturing Electronic Voice Phenomena (EVP) on audiotape, is the most substantial treatment of this topic that I know of. The Wikipedia entries on Raudive and EVP give results and brief critiques of studies conducted by several scientific researchers into this odd phenomenon.

Two Gallons of Drinking Water (1999)

Lake Canandaigua, New York: At my third Dzogchen meditation retreat with Lama Surya Das. I keep a two gallon plastic container of drinking water in my room, which I impulsively decide to give to the folks that run the retreat office. So I carry the container into the office on my shoulder, set it down, and am met with looks of astonishment. One of the staff members there says, "We were just talking a minute ago about how we wished we had a two gallon water container like this for the office. Thank you."

Seen from the Ledge of Sleep (2000)

I'm lying in bed after several days of heavy rain. I wonder whether the downpour's worn away much soil from the steep stream-bank of the creek at Wilson Park, about three miles away. It's a place I've often visited and sometimes found flint artifacts and shards. From the ledge of sleep, that edge that borders on rest and reverie, I'm suddenly staring at two broad flint pieces, now half exposed by earth-eroding rain. They weren't visible at all a week or so before when I actually walked by Wilson Creek. Later that same day, the cloud cover lifts, and I drive over to the park and walk down to the steep spot by the creek where vision blossomed as I'd lain in bed. Right where I'd peered through inner windows of perception are two half-buried atl atl points, both broken, broad flint pieces which come gladly to my hand.

As intriguing as such externally occurring events are in themselves, beneath them I sense an even more significant communion which benefits both me and the land itself. This kind of experience of salutary oneness with a well known and loved location is something I've written poems about over the years. Here's one that touches on the topic in an imaginative fashion:

Guardians

As we drove toward Council Grove,
I thought (seeing darkness deep
in a morning window) living there
is one who, caved into himself
at night, becomes winds
rivering through cottonwoods
across Kansas, nameless guardian
of stream banks and gullies.

And later as we turned into
Wakeeny, I felt brush past me
hints of one who holds
the entire sway of grasses on this plain.
Prayers appearing in their sheen
open in her mind
as she sits in a porch swing,
somewhere near the trembling of roads.

We headed West through crosswinds,
past wheat's gold inscriptions,
spying traces in that tall afternoon
of one who wheels across cumulus
on wings of red-tailed hawks,
scattering visions like rain
on the earth below.

From a distant farmhouse,
walled in a windbreak,
broodings rose up at twilight
of one who wears the wet
weave of roots gently as her own veins,
siphoning life into their outstretched branches.

So on the unsheltered plain,
each soul that wakens
in its cradle of flesh,
aligns with space,
and is drawn out into the guardianship
of what it loves most deeply.

John Locke Dies as I Try to Reach Him (2000)

My friend, Dr. John R. Locke, is the Founder and Director of the Department of Comparative Literature at the University of Arkansas. A tremendously popular teacher beloved by many in our community, he also is a scholarly author, a translator of Rilke and other poets, himself a poet, and a dedicated practitioner of Buddhist meditation. John's a man of manifold sensitivities, and a mentor to many younger people. Like me.

I rarely call him, but on August 28, 2000, I feel a strong urge to be in touch, and phone his number at the University of Arkansas. I'm greeted by a secretary in the office who tells me in a hushed, greatly agitated tone that John is in his office with a student advisee. At this point, I hear a gun shot. As far as I've been able to determine, this is the second time the student fires on John. The third shot kills him.

Moments later, the disturbed student turns his gun on himself, and blows himself away with two more bullets. The entire campus community and John's large circle of friends are shocked and deeply grieved. I'm asked to present a eulogy for him at the memorial service, which gives me the opportunity to share some of his poetry. I subsequently pen a poem for Dr. Locke myself, an exact transcription of a dream-vision in which I see the poem as a lofty, luminous tree with a column of words superimposed upon its ascending trunk. I clearly hear these words intoned at the same time that I read them. The poem is a meditation on the seamless continuity of life and death, and the Wholeness that holds them both:

Dream Tree Poem

In Memory of John Locke

This is written as a tree
completely swathed in gauzy
energy rears its bare limbs
and climbs up through the filmy
blue solution of the sky.
In this kinetic photograph,
the nimbus round the branches
flames like ever-burning fuel.
A narrative is heard that's
also written, consonantal with
the plunge of tree trunk,
thus: "In friends, the Higher
Life is fed by those who die,
and that life lasts as
it adds life to all those
friends who still live on.
Can the tree itself be
strengthened by the joy in
this exchange? I don't know,
but..." Here the words fade
out, but in the living image
"those who die" are present
as dead branches on the tree.
The whitish incandescence
licks round them undiminished
on the page. Then suddenly
the dream's completely gone,
leaving only
native joy.

In Haunts of Ancient Power (2001)

Inside West Kennett Long Barrow

*(Large burial mound, Marlborough Downs, England,
built c. 3600 BC and in use until c. 2200 BC)*

Gravity of mass graves tugs me down
into a musty meditative stupor.
As I sink and settle, a presence penetrates me--
fierce, vigilant, yet finally permissive.
It shapeshifts, unfettered by corporeal form:
warrior, raptor, bear...
This is very close to be to death,
but I allow the energy entry,
am briefly overshadowed,
then return to personhood.
I rise on trembling legs, and resurface
out the vaginal exit of the grassy mound.

I'm here with Leslie and our daughter Amy. I emerge from the
mound to find Amy in conversation with a wild-haired boy who
tells us that he camped here the night before and was disturbed
by a presence that he sensed came from the Long Barrow. Peter
Knight, a researcher of ancient sites in the U.K., has written a book
titled <u>West Kennet Long Barrow: Landscapes, Shamans and the
Cosmos</u> (2011) which includes many reports of individuals' psychic experiences there.

West Kennett Long Barrow is an underground burial site located in a farmer's field near manmade Silbury Hill, the immense
Avebury stone circle, and other early Celtic ceremonial earthworks. This is one of the areas with the highest concentration of
crop circles in Britain, and the world. Jeffrey Wilson, director of the
Independent Crop Circle Researcher's Association (www.iccra.org),

an organization of American researchers, said in a teleconference lecture I heard in 2011 that a majority of crop circles in both the U.K. and the U.S. have appeared near such ancient earthworks. About 65% of the approximately seven hundred such circles that have been documented in the U.S. since 1847 have been proximate to Native American sites like the Serpent Mound and the Miamisburg Mound (which resembles the conical Silbury Hill) in Ohio.

Over ten thousand of these precise, mathematically fascinating and suggestive designs (or signs!) have been found in fields in the U.K.. They have become increasingly intricate and beautiful over the decades. Since the time of the ancient Greeks, only ten solutions have been found to the classic geometrical problem of how to square a circle. In the U.S., a crop design found in a field near the Serpent Mound has repaid study by eliciting two more entirely new solutions to the problem.

Researchers in the field (no pun intended) of "cereology," or the physical analysis of the crops that are somehow bent down to form these designs, have found unnaturally elongated growth nodes and "expulsion cavities" (holes blown out at the nodes). Readings conducted by Geiger counter, magnetometer, and EM devices, as well as plant and soil testing, reveal phenomena that these researchers consider "unhoaxable" anomalies. For a detailed verbal and photographic consideration of these phenomena, see www.bltresearch.com/plantab.php. For a searching study of the effects of crop circles on water samples and different systems in our bodies, including alterations in brain waves, see the website of distinguished English researcher Lucy Pringle, a founding member of the Centre for Crop Circle Studies.

Crop circles are cropping up (pun intended) all over the world, not just in our country and the U.K.. I am very curious about the possible connection between energetically charged places like the West Kennett Long Barrow and these designs. I certainly have felt a powerful energy inside the Long Barrow on the two visits I've made there, and wonder how such energies might relate or contribute to the evidently intelligent forces which create these mysterious living symbols.

Further On Down the Line (2001)

St. Nectan's Glen

(Near Tintagel, Cornwall)

1.
Holy waters wash past
hurts away; grant us
ease today.

> Here today, gone today--
> the stream never returns.
> It's ever current, ever new.

We're recalled
to gladness
in this glade.

> Nectar of presence,
> freshets of praise
> gush from St. Nectan's Glen.

2.
    We sit in meditation in St. Nectan's hermit cell. My awareness suddenly shifts about two hundred miles to the northeast. I don't know how I know this, but it's visual and vivid, a brief relocation. Later we speak with the custodian of the place, who tells us that major ley lines run from St. Michael's Mount in southwest Cornwall through St. Nectan's cell itself, then on through Glastonbury, and further on about two hundred miles to the northeast--an "Old Straight Track" or energetic Interstate. I've evidently been transported.

The term "ley lines" in the above two-part poem refers to ancient neolithic "trackways" in the U.K. which were created to facilitate overland treks. These "old straight tracks" are still discernible in the landscape. A second, more esoteric meaning of the phrase denotes energetic pathways thought to stretch between prominent hilltops, megalithic monuments and stone circles. Since our visit to Britain in 2001, I have found several references to ley lines which are said to pass through St.Nectan's Glen.

Predictive IG (2001)

Denver, Colorado: I call my inner guidance "IG." Often before or during times of travel, I'll rest back and ask IG for information that might allow me more sense of direction or clarity about the journey. In this instance, I'm wondering about an upcoming retreat held by the extraordinary spiritual group Waking Down in Mutuality, an essential resource for me from the year 2000 on. And IG gives me all sorts of information, including a most cryptic phrase, "Randy's going to bring his music." This is puzzling, since I don't know of any Randy in our group. Yet, on arrival at the YMCA Camp at Estes Park, Colorado where the retreat is to be held, a fellow named Randy shows up with a boom box loaded with all kinds of CDs which he shares regularly on breaks and in the evenings after the scheduled programs are over. Randy's presence at the event doesn't feel random to me at all!

"Let Peace Branch Between Us" (2001)

One of my eco-spiritual heroines is Julia Butterfly Hill, the brave young woman who sat for 738 days in a redwood tree she named Luna to protect it and other California redwoods from logging by the Pacific Lumber Company. Formerly a native of my home town, Julia returned to Fayetteville in 2000 to speak at the University of Arkansas about what she had learned during her long tree-sitting sojourn. Her talk raised my consciousness about the importance of preserving forests of ancient giants like Luna, and about the soulful relationships that can develop between humans and individual trees. Within a year of hearing Julia speak, I camped out by the Cossatot River in Arkansas, and had a surprising experience of connection with the trees there, described in the following poem:

124

For the Trees and Julia Butterfly Hill

Once I camped out
in an Ozark river valley,
and felt the creeping sense
of something very wrong,
some kind of shady deal gone down.
Curious, I tuned in to the trees
and received a jolt of sad distress,
accompanied by the words
"GET POLITICAL."
I didn't understand this message.
Yet.

When morning came,
I walked over the hill-rise
to an savage clear cut.
My eyes seared at the sight
of what had upset my sleep
all night: the loss, the tear
of so many branching songs
gone.

Oh trees,
how can we protect you?
How do we infuse heart
into our politics
and grassroots actions?

The trees stay, minding and mending
the whole scene; not patient
but present.
Walt Whitman wrote it:

all the while, they're
"uttering joyous leaves,"
exuding crucial oxygen.

Oh trees,
let peace branch between us again.

Just as our beloved pets or the birds that gather at our back yard birdbaths and feeders can open us to a heightened awareness of the natural world, the experience of developing a relationship with a particular tree is one of the most common and accessible ways by which people discover the promise of direct communion with an aspect of Nature. The little poem below is a celebration of one such relationship, which I've found to be consistently grounding and calming. It's addressed directly to my tree-friend:

OAK ANGEL

Tree at our window
presiding Oak
you stand before me
a branching of brown roads
and tell me my roots
cannot fail thirst
for in the earth
our life is.
Old angel
you were singing

in the crush of day
as you are now
in the rose church
of twilight
but only now I hear.
While we sleep
you walk
the deep world-breezes--
night's cool hand
on the brow of our city.

Inner Laughter Heard (2001)

Fayetteville: Since 1995, I've led weekly meetings of the Buddhist Meditation and Spiritual Support Group. I'm now ready for a break, and arrange to be temporarily spelled by another regular leader, a capable, highly intelligent fellow named Stephen. I announce to the group that I'm passing the torch of leadership on to him, then we all meditate. During the meditation, I see a pen (maybe it's a golden one; maybe it's writing by itself--I forget the details) and hear loud male laughter in my mind. After the meditation, I share this, and it turns out that Stephen has also heard loud male laughter in his mind during the sitting. No other members of the group hear this.

"Hi" Drama (2002)

Ojai, California: At a retreat at the Matilija Springs Retreat Center outside Ojai, with big odiferous eucalyptus trees, gigantic twisty oak, the gush of a fast creek, and about forty other aspirants on the spiritual path. I'm attending a week-long Waking Down in Mutuality (WDM) retreat. Today, the whole group meets to meditate. I sit near Bob, a man I've been in close rapport with, and gradually drop more deeply into silence.

The group is very still, collectively submerged. All at once, my mind opens into a clear felt sense of sheer awareness. It's like my head has popped up to the surface and I'm seeing sunshine and breathing fresh air. Concurrent with this moment, I hear Saniel Bonder, the founder of WDM, say "Hi, Geoff." I assume he's greeting me from his well-established inherency in Spirit, to acknowledge my own sudden recognition of same.

Right after the meditation, I mention this fleeting "Hi, Geoff" to Saniel. He assures me that he didn't speak, as does at least one other participant. But my buddy Bob tells me that he also heard Saniel say those two words loud and clear.

"Spring Storm" by Robert Sudlow (1995)

Going for the Gnome Rock in the Rain (2002)

I'm driving in the Flint Hills of central eastern Kansas in the rain. I'm passing sloping fields near Matfield Green, when suddenly I know I have to stop. Something impels me to get out of the car and cross a high wet field of native grasses in search of a fieldstone I can sense I'm being led to like a dog follows a scent to some unseen den. By this time, the rain's pummeling down so hard my glasses are like beaded watery curtains.

At the field's far reach, I see a dull, rain-polished grey shape protruding from the earth and know by intuition that it's the rock I've come for. Not stopping to examine it, I lift it from its half-enveloping cradle in the limestone-studded soil, wrap it in a small soft blanket, place it gently on the backseat of my car, and begin the drive back south, well-satisfied to carry home a piece of the Flint Hills.

A day or so of travel, then I'm home, and in due time I lift the mystery rock from out its swaddling blanket. It's shocking--an almost exact limestone replica of a stone garden gnome that's graced twenty years of gardens at both houses where we've lived in Fayetteville. I mean almost exactly exact, the same sixteen inch high size, the peaked cap, the leftward lean, the outlined shape of arms and cupped proto-hands...amazing. The two stones stand companionably near each other in our garden, a twin testimony to the powers of intuition and to the magic that lurks close to the earth in dens and bones and wind-and-water-contoured stones.

Poetic Present (2003)

At another Waking Down in Mutuality retreat, I find myself in a small group with a professional musician, a frequent performer and established recording artist. She's somewhat slow to share in the group, but we two gradually develop a measure of rapport, and during a free afternoon while browsing in a bookstore in a town near the retreat center, I see a slim volume of poetry by a little-known poet which I am unaccountably drawn to purchase as a gift for her.

When our group reconvenes, I give her the book, and her jaw drops in complete surprise. It turns out that she's just finished a performance of some poems which had been set to music from this very book, and has since been wanting to obtain a copy and read it in its entirety. After this synchronicity, she warms further to me and seems to be more emotionally open in the group.

My Brother Dies (2003)

I fall asleep and am suddenly caught up in a semi-lucid dream state in headlong, panicked flight from church to church in what seems to be downtown Kansas City. I look in through church windows, then rapidly fly on. I even peer through the window of a Buddhist place of worship. (Some months later, I actually see this building, which houses the Rime Buddhist Center in downtown Kansas City.) I'm fearful, propelled forward by forces beyond my understanding. I end up floating near the ceiling of a large, dark, musty room, thinking that this must be what it's like to be a confused, earthbound ghost.

Another baffling aspect of this dream experience involves a struggle to breathe, which begins to make sense to me when I learn the next morning from my mother that at the time I had the dream, my brother choked in his sleep--a combination of sleep apnea and congestive heart failure--then fell out of bed and died on the floor of his apartment in Kansas City.

I'm left with questions: Did I take on some of the distress he experienced while dying? Was this highly unusual dream in any way helpful to him? I hadn't known my brother was about to die, but I had sensed the possibility as much as two or three weeks prior. We spoke on the phone less than a week before his death, and at that time, he said, "I love you," to me three times with extreme sweetness as we told each other goodbye. That turned out to be our very last goodbye.

Two Vehicles, Bumper to Bumper, Abandoned by Two Women Drivers (2004)

I'm considering a trip to California, and as I usually do before making plane reservations and other travel plans, I seek inner guidance about the rightness of my timing. I fall asleep and dream I'm driving on a freeway in a big yellow school bus, chugging along in the fast lane. Then I must stop quickly, and do, just in time to avert a collision with two cars, abandoned bumper to bumper, which I somehow know were driven by two women who have left them there.

I wake and my interpretation of the dream is: take it easy on this trip--i.e., stay out of the fast lane! I figure my anima will appreciate the slowed-down pace of a good vacation. But first, before I go traipsing off west, Leslie and I decide to visit my mother in Kansas City. We pack and get ready to go, and right then Mom calls us to report that my dear cousin Gerda is in the hospital, most likely hours from death. The timing is striking; we're able to instantly hop in the car and drive up to Kansas City. I meet my mother at the hospital there. Gerda's eyes are glazed, but she sees that I've arrived. A smile plays on her lips, then she closes her eyes as I begin to slowly stroke her brow over and over again with great tenderness. I am inviting her to rest, and to let go. My mother sits there watching as I stroke Gerda's brow like this for about an hour.

Gerda never opens her eyes again. When Mom and I go out to get some lunch, she quietly dies. My mother's final obligation to another person is completed, but now she's dreading all the stressful work a funeral entails. I offer to say a brief five minute eulogy at Gerda's funeral, but to my surprise Mom says, intensely, "No"! At least twenty minutes!" This will take a lot of work to pull together, but I recall an interview that I'd taped with Gerda a few years back about her childhood in Posnen, Poland. Once back home in Arkansas, I listen to the interview and craft a thoughtful, heartfelt eulogy at least twenty minutes long.

I'm oddly agitated, anxious the whole week prior to the funeral service. At one point, I break down in tears and tell Leslie, "When my mother dies, I don't want to be the one to do the eulogy for her." I can't account for how stressed I feel. My mother is very wrought up about all the little details to be dealt with, as well. During the same week, our daughter Amy finds a button that reads "I Love Grandma" near her college dorm, and draws the button in a doodle in her journal. And one of Amy's closest friends dreams that she is crying over the loss of a relative.

The day arrives (Friday the 13th) and off we go to Beard's Funeral Chapel, where my father's then my brother's services were held as well. Mourners arrive, and I soon rise and begin to speak. I voice my appreciation of my mother's care for Gerda in a few well-chosen sentences early in the talk, and speaking on, am just barely aware as Mom leaves the room. I'm so focused on carrying out her wishes that I'm again only peripherally aware when a little later Leslie also leaves the room, along with one other woman whose name I don't know.

As I conclude the eulogy, Leslie re-enters the chapel and says, "Geoff, you'd better come with me, something's happened to your mother." I quickly walk back to a little side room where the unknown woman (who turns out to be a nurse) attends my mom, whose color is very pale. Mom sees me, then just after that, exactly as with Gerda the week before, she shuts her eyes, and never opens them again. The ambulance arrives and takes her to the hospital emergency room, where tests are taken and a kindly, honest doctor tells us that she's suffered a massive stroke and has about an hour to live.

We're given a curtained-off area. I've never pictured being with my relatives at any of their deaths, except my mom. I stroke her forehead and tell her that she can let go. The doctor tells me she very probably can hear, though not respond, and since this would be her last unmet concern, I reassure her that we'll find a good home for Tenzy, her little Lhasa Apso Terrier. Phone calls aren't supposed to be allowed in this quiet space, but suddenly a phone rings by my mother's bed, and a friend who Leslie has briefly contacted with the news about my mother calls to say a home's been found for Tenzy. We don't know why or how the hospital let that call through, but we share the news with Mom. Her last obligation's met! Soon she passes peacefully--the second woman to leave her earthly vehicle--so soon, so close behind the first, my cousin Gerda.

Many people have noticed a proliferation of synchronicities and signs of communication with the "other side" both prior to and after someone passes away. Leslie and I experience additional synchronicities in the days after Mom's death. We also receive a distinct sense of her presence: as Leslie sits with my mother's body, she sees a kind of mandala of my mother and father ice-skating joyfully around in a circle, finally reunited. Soon after, she learns that my parents always loved skating together. In the evening after Mom's death, I have a vision of her gazing into my eyes, which is followed by a near-lucid dream in which I find myself in a rarified, high alpine setting. The earth there is covered with crystals emanating rainbow light. We find some solace and inspiration in these apparent intuitions of reunion and presence.

Oh Where Oh Where Has My Little Dog Gone? (2006)

We're on the dock of a place we share with friends at Beaver Lake, near the Arkansas-Missouri border. Our dog Bosco, a handsome, perky little Pomeranian, scurries uphill toward the house. Suddenly, we hear a strangled yelp, and I tear up the path to find our neighbor's Jack Russell terrier with his jaws clamped around Bosco's neck. He dies in Leslie's lap shortly thereafter.

A few hours later, I sit upstairs and am swept by an impression of an 'expanded version' of Bosco; very noble, valiant and dashing, a bit like a small furry caped superhero. Love pours through my heart in loyal torrents.

Leslie's sitting downstairs, so I immediately go down to tell her of this unexpected experience. She meets me with a look of awe and tells me she's just now felt a tremendous wave of love, both for and somehow from our fuzzy little maybe-out-of-body buddy. Is this synchronicity, telepathy, or truly direct contact?   Though we may never know for sure, we're uplifted and somewhat comforted.

Hearts of Stone (2006–2011)

I begin to find one perfectly heart-shaped stone after another in my roamings along the chert-bright shores at Beaver Lake, and in many other locations around the continent. A consistent pattern reveals itself: I walk and pray and radiate my affection to the earth, and frequently right after reaching the halfway point or the very end of my hike, or instantly after leaving a special offering to the local spirits of Nature, the very next thing I spy is one of these valentines from Gaia. The sustained level of synchronicity is astonishing to me, and it conveys a felt sense of heartful connection with the natural world.

Robert Sudlow and the Clod from God (2007)

Robert Sudlow was a Kansas landscape painter who died in March, 2010 at age 90. I met him when I was fifteen. Bob is the most important male spiritual friend of my life. His paintings and drawings illustrate this book. They are ever suggestive of merging--presence of earthsky as a fused "unity of two." (You can go to www.robertsudlow.com to see a generous sampling of his magnificent oil paintings and lithographs.)

Bob's art and some of his journal writings are also reproduced in two books, <u>Landscapes in Kansas, Paintings by Robert Sudlow</u> (1987) and <u>Spiritual Journeys, The Art of Robert Sudlow</u> (2002). Additionally, many of his journal-cum-sketch books are archived at the Spencer Art Museum at the University of Kansas in Lawrence and can be viewed there (www. spencerart.ku.edu).

The entries in his journals reflect Bob's bone deep communion with the Earth. He made many of these notations outdoors after painting, in a swervy scrawl that just quivers with Being. Reading them, one senses that as Bob painted, he was frequently ambushed and eclipsed by the Sacred.

Robert Sudlow's keen, ecstatic observations of both outer and his own interior landscapes go on page after page, book after journal book, for decades, the pages all brocaded with his deft sketches and augmented with passages from favorite writers. Here are some excerpts gleaned from two journals he kept from May, 1997 until January, 1999. Just as most of the prose in this book is set in the present tense, he mostly writes about what is happening right now, "eternally now: "

May 4, 1997:

A late pale blush before night. A moment of exhalation, a long release of breath. Earth still: returning its afternoon warmth into hovering air--tiny insects rising, invisible thronging life, shadows silent, growing more dense--the whippoorwill...a web of place, season, and hour when the observer becomes absorbed in space.

Farm lights become stars on the hills. Transitional states I would paint in the midst of change, whirl in the ambiences.

It seems that in recall I most recognize the approach of a sacred presence, a moment my dream is so natural, so transparent that it is not marked--a door has been opened unobtrusively enlarging and bringing peace simply by being available.

September 25, 1997:

Bright clarity. Gold-flecked, blue stained hills. A dream: honey-pitted, golden color that would cure mortality. Be very still and surrender this body to death--leave the temporary for the season of all seasons. Beneath all actions of men lies stillness: a lot of noise ending in silence. Keep that treasure. Radiance in the sunlight. Monarchs on the move, high gliding southward. We all seek dominance in this playground. All would be winners. The stars are mocking us. Remember me on gravestones. Beads of rain still glisten on tree stems. Intricate simplicity, a shining surface, facets of dreaming, plumage of glory.

September 28, 1997:

A world in constant movement. At night I hear the spheres turn. Today breezes play and monarchs sail. All is transparent and adrift. As new as Eden, the sunlight penetrates to our bones. The sky is opened, smiling and carefree. Darkness is conquered.

October 23, 1997:

A quilted sky, lambs wool overhead. A vivid sparkling morning, promisingly pure. The dog is chewing on a stick. Few leaves falling. The valley humming with life, abundance, ripeness, and serene joy. I sense sounds beyond hearing, lights surpassing eyesight, and the scent of ineffable blooms.

An infinitely detailed tapestry--my rug and yours.

...A deep breathing earth becomes my companion. A respiration shared when boundaries are down. Rooted trees move in a warm wind, a passing that tells of a common existence now whenever I pause.

Undated, sometime in August, 1998:

A preference for stillness and nonhuman voices, cries and whispers of unseen critters--perhaps sounds that come before language: unshaped vowels of original wildness--the wind through dark foliage and the call of screech owl simply here--randomness and chance, a firefly on this page. All moments made new--palpable breath merged with night.

The original matrix. Indeterminate passage. Fullness, weight and glory. Begin again. A continuation of the past. Absent present. Present future. Present past. Future present.

...All my seasons are one in silence.

September 19, 1998:

My introduction into waking becomes both a loss and a gain. Alone in dreams I participate across all boundaries (both as an actor and observer). Waking early, I become embodied in time. Possibilities abound, as in childhood. There freedom is sensed. Yet the day, by becoming measure, becomes time--a linear sequence beginning and ending with choices and erasures. Innocence settles into self-consciousness...The horizon becomes closer. Names replace dreams.

September 21, 1998:

The Kingdom of Heaven is spread across the earth-- Now. Not in some future tense, not in the golden past, but now, eternally now.

Awake.

Slow and in solemn majesty, thrones and dominions move in the morning rain clouds.

...We see consecutively, scene following scene, when actually the view is continuous, seamlessly present-- often all at once.

November 16, 1998 [*written when Bob was painting in the Flint Hills, near Matfield Green, Kansas*]:

...The old Rogler house...wind blowing across flat prairie, sounding through grasses, pummeling my ears--carrying the music of distant crows. Long cloud strands unwind and are strewn beyond sight...Oaks prevail--thriving and heavy-armed guardians rooted deep, scarcely touched by the autumn wind.

Joyous morning on the Cottonwood [*my note: Cottonwood Creek, which runs through the old Rogler ranch*] ...Accidents happen. Set the stage and let them have their way. My canvas blooms by itself.

...Geoff departs and leaves gifts...We ran parallel for a little while, our effect on each other quite out of time.

The way Bob lived and worked inspired me to offer adoration and praise back to Nature. For him painting was a sacramental act, partaking of a very similar spirit to be found in Jesuit priest and paleontologist Pierre Teilhard de Chardin's great text <u>The Mass on the World</u>, (written 1918-1923) in which, while traveling in the steppes of Asia without Communion wine or wafers, de Chardin makes the whole earth his altar and offers it up for divinization (in Greek, *theosis*), blessing the entire planet.

When I was with Bob as he painted outdoors, I could feel the way his loving attention saturated the landscape. His powerful unitive influence lifted me "quite out of time. " I tried to describe his eternalizing impact on me in this poem:

He Paints With Me

I walk through one of Sudlow's paintings,
through the landscape *as* he paints it.
I feel fineness, brushed by vast awareness.
I walk as Bob works on a hill
of golden prairie grasses grazed by wind.
I feel inscape; invoked into the scene
he's working on and in, into the sphere
where his attention dilates.

"Inscape" is a word coined by the poet Gerard Manley Hopkins' (1844-1889). It denotes the unique nature or essence of a specific person, place, or thing. Hopkins saw and felt the sacred essence of each object in the landscape. His poetry attests this sense of inscape, always:

"The world is charged with the Grandeur of God.
    It will flame out, like shining from shook foil."

(from the poem "God's Grandeur")

Robert Sudlow was so intimate with the inscape of eastern Kansas that being in the field with him facilitated some remarkable confirmatory experiences and communions of my own. Let's slide a few years back in time... Bob takes me to a hillside farm where he's done a lot of outdoor painting in all kinds of weather. We're walking through the center of a field which he says has recently been further cleared and expanded by bulldozing. I vaguely sense a disturbance here, and ask Bob, "Do you think that the Nature spirits get upset by things like this clearing that's just been done?"

Bob's walking about eight feet in front of me. There are no trees; nothing above us or anywhere near us. Immediately after I ask him that question, a solid dirt clod falls out of thin air from directly above me and hits me smack on the chest right over my heart. I check with Bob that he hasn't mischievously tossed it back over his shoulder, but no, he hasn't. I'm inclined to take this as a direct answer from Nature, and feel it couldn't have happened without Bob's potentiating connection with the living energies of this cherished place where he's painted so often.

Kansas Browns

For Robert Sudlow

I know a quiet artist who likes to paint farmers' fields
late afternoons in autumn, then sit with evening
colors and smoke a nicked old pipe.

Kansas smells of goldenrod, walnuts, baled hay, rain,
ploughed ground, soybeans, clay banks, limestone
creek beds, "and something of the color brown,"
he says. "Smells best in mid-fall..."

Then, hedge apples are last to drop.
They cluster pale green near the fence posts,
filled with thick milk beneath their pulp.

Mild cows stand stalled at gates,
by troughs and ponds, heaving
steady breaths.

The artist holds a palette swirled with Kansas browns
of shady forest deer-paths, furrows, umber gaps.
At dusk he puts his brush and palette down.
We sit in evening fields.

"You Who Are High with the Angels" (2008)

Fountain Hills, Arizona: I'm seated next to my father-in-law
on a sofa in his apartment at a residential care facility. He's been in
gradual decline for some time, and has taken to catching short cat-
nips while sitting up. As he naps, I use the opportunity to silently
pray for him, hoping that he'll be receptive to angelic healing and
peace during this interval of rest. As I attune to healing angels on
his behalf, in his sleep Sidney asks out loud, "And you, you who
are high with the angels, how do you..." His words trail off into
silence. And that's the only time I ever hear him mention angels,
or speak to me in his sleep, during the entire thirty-eight years I
know my father-in-law.

Now the Circle Is Unbroken (2008)

Fayetteville: Leslie's and my friend and musical partner Nick is
dying of a fast-onset form of multiple sclerosis. I feed him the last
bite of food he chooses to take in--a forkful of mascarpone cheese-
cake. Eating is no longer enjoyable. His body is finally ready to
let go, and his soul ready to finally fly. Now another day or two
passes without his eating or drinking, and friends gather around
at his home outside town to support Nick and his wife Ginny, as he
approaches the portal between this life and the next.

I'm not present among those friends the night Nick finally dies,
at least not physically. For some time I've had a ticket to go hear
the great American jazz pianist and composer Mose Allison play
in Fayetteville, so now I sit in a concert hall, digging Mose's musical mosaic of jazzy tunes and great whimsical lyrics. At the same

time, I multi-track, slipping away in consciousness--once about ten minutes into the concert, and later about forty minutes thereafter-- to check in on and bless the unfoldment of Nick's dying.

Without knowing the degree of accuracy of my perceptions, the first time I drop in on the deathbed scene I sense a circle of love and awareness around Nick's bed, extending perhaps one hundred feet above his home. But the circle has distinct boundaries, and something seems unfinished, still contained and held in abeyance.

When I re-check and re-bless forty minutes or so later, I receive a distinct impression of the same numinous circle, but now it's full of a new buoyancy, and it radiates outward and upward without any boundaries. What was contained is now free to move out, and I unexpectedly hear a joyful surge of music with the words: "Now the circle is unbroken." My hunch is that Nick has passed over.

Returning to awareness of the concert, I enjoy Mose's last few tunes, then drive quickly home and phone Nick's house. A mutual friend tells me that he passed at almost exactly the time of my second "fly-by." She adds that as Nick's vital signs ceased, the many friends gathered around his bed broke into the old country gospel tune "May The Circle Be Unbroken," singing our dear friend on his way into the kindly Light.

Looking Back

The long period between 1989-2009 was one of the most active times of my life to date, in terms of fruitful self-exploration and growthful connection with others. Those two threads of my experience--the personal and the mutual--became more finely woven with each other, as the inner work I accomplished made it possible for me to offer more of myself to my clients, co-workers, and family. I have more years to look back on in this summary than in any of the others. The following synopsis provides some context for the stories I've shared in this chapter:

Professionally, I practiced psychotherapy and massage therapy with clients from all kinds of backgrounds and worked on psychiatric units as a music therapist. I received training in a host of therapeutic approaches, and refined both my verbal skills and intuition as I conducted many sessions of clinical hypnosis. I've learned so much from my clients about our vast, often unexplored resources for growth and healing.

Artistically, I published two books of poetry and released two CDs of original songs during this time. I began leading poetry writing groups, and doing poetry therapy with a few literary minded clients. It was a special joy to begin to bring my creative and therapeutic work together in this way.

Personally, Leslie and I went from being the parents of our two young children to full empty nest status during these years--a truly heart-opening journey! My brother and both of my parents died during this chapter of my life, and I became the elder of my family line. My friendship with Robert Sudlow evolved during this time. His celebratory communion with the earth kept rubbing off on me, over the days we spent together at his Kansas home and the places where he painted.

Some people don't want or need to do incisive psychospiritual work. For me, it's been necessary for full, well-grounded development and productive work in the world. I spent over six years in Jungian and body-based Hakomi psychotherapy from the late eighties to the mid-nineties, which helped me drop down into painful emotional shadow material that had sorely needed my attention but required expert support to address.

In 1990, my meditation practice became more serious and I began participating in frequent retreats with great Tibetan and American Buddhist teachers. The helpful experience of meditating with others at these retreats led me to found a weekly Buddhist Meditation and Spiritual Support Group in 1995. This lively free group has been well-attended and is now being facilitated by six rotating leaders. In 2008, I began spiritual study with the brilliant Buddhist teacher Anna Cox, whose Dharma Friends Prison Outreach Project on behalf of prisoners in Arkansas and across the country is an enormous source of inspiration for many of these most marginalized members of our society.

In 2000, I connected with the pioneering spiritual group Waking Down in Mutuality (WDM), which has provided rock solid, trustworthy support for my personal and transpersonal development. Intensive work with my WDM teacher and friend Sandra Glickman precipitated a significant spiritual shift in 2002. Since 2005, I've offered support to others in WDM as a mentor.

Along with the above involvements, I contacted David Spangler in 2002, and began studying Incarnational Spirituality through his courses at the Lorian Association website. I also made occasional visits to Lorian's home base in western Washington State. Lorian and David offer skillful, convivial spiritual support through their educational programs and publications. My stays at the Findhorn Community during my student year in Scotland ended just a month or so before David arrived there. It's been fulfilling to revitalize my bond with the extended Findhorn world-community through my relationship with Lorian, and a short visit to Findhorn which Leslie and I made in 2006.

So what did I learn from all these inner and outer doings? The spiritual teacher and author A. H. Almaas writes of an "optimizing force" in us all, an evolutionary tropism or tendency toward greater wholeness. I've learned that we can say an internal "yes" to this force. With patience over time, our assent can bring us into more complete alignment with our life purpose, growing the fullness of our unique incarnation and gifts. Saying that "yes" made some space for magic in my midlife years.

VII. Recent Findings and Openings

Christic Cup (2010)

I visit my devoutly Christian friend Gloria Okes Perkins to discuss and appreciate poems from her new book <u>After Eden,</u> and to request her to pray with me that I might receive the spirit of Christ more deeply. During our period of wordless prayer, I see a tall grail cup overflowing with white light, which is simultaneously Christ's radiant body, its arms outstretched downward in blessing. I take the cup and drink its dazzling contents down, and prayer-light shines inside me.

After we begin speaking again, Gloria tells me that during the silence she has "heard" a message she feels is meant for me: "Take of this cup and drink to your heart's content." I'm moved to share a love poem here:

"This Mystery, Which Is Christ in You, The Hope of Glory"

(Colossians 1:27)

He fell down the sky
in a raiment of bone,
the Babe born
in the wild-rose womb
of Mary.
He brings down dew,
cool balm for the thirst
of the prisoner
chained through ages
of starlight.

Babylon may fall,

arise again,
fall,
but the waking head
in the Light
does not perish.
Inward blossoms,
inward spring
are ours.

Behind a mental door of ice,
a world of original beings
strives for Him.
Leave this room,
filled with the artifacts
of winter.
Beyond the rocky shore
the sea washes in
indelible clouds
of flowers,
an earthly room
sanctified.

Button, Button (2011)

I'm home, cleaning feverishly, after finally getting over a hell of a fever, which turned into a life-threatening systemic infection that got me hospitalized for five days. Now, as I scour out a drawer in our bathroom, I automatically toss a little black button into the already burgeoning waste basket. Immediately after doing this, I remember the way the Irish offer coins and buttons to the faery folk in wild places, such as remote burial mounds and springs. I regret letting that button go, and think to begin a reconnaissance mission to pick through all the stuff in the stuffed waste basket and find it. But the task looks daunting, and results uncertain, so I abandon the search and forge ahead with my drawer-clearing project.

Several days later, after the waste basket has been emptied and the floor swept and mopped, I walk back into our bathroom and there's the same black button sitting solo on the tile floor a few feet from that very drawer. No other item of the multitude of small scraps and bits of trash from my fast cleaning foray remain, but somehow, the button has turned up again, and I take it outside right away and offer it to the faery (aka "fey" or "fay" folk) of this part of Fayetteville. Placing it in a part of our garden we've devoted to their presence and pleasure, I shake my head in wonder and wonder, "Now what were the chances of that happening?"

We Think Along the Same Green Lines (2011)

One evening in early spring, after planting kale and mixed mesclun greens seeds in our garden, I lie abed in a reverie about green vegetables--the look of sleek new greens; the taste of moist, rain-fattened leaves on my imaginal tongue. I'm loving all this beautiful green soul food, when Leslie enters the waking-dream-drenched room. I tell her I've been picturing spring greens, and she exclaims that she's just been engaged in the same exact contemplation. We feel that flash of deep connective joy that comes when this kind of sensitivity suddenly reveals itself, and we feel held by what is always holding us, the ground and Ground of Being, the greens-to-be, the whole sweet seamless scene.

We like to pick edible wild greens from our lawn and eat vegetables from our garden and winter cold-frame. As much as possible, we buy locally grown vegetables from our farmer's market and food co-op. This is grassroots activism--the kind that activates healthy local sustainability and community; the kind one can savor and feel grateful for! Because we become what we eat over time, eating a high quality organic diet can help us embody more of Nature's living power. A healthy diet makes it easier to cope with our chemically toxic environment and to connect and resonate with Nature.

From the very earliest plantings at our current house, the Nature spirits in our gardens have beckoned back to us. One spring day in 1997, I attune to them as the first mixed greens are just coming up. Sitting in an easy chair in a room with a good view of the garden, I relax back and slip into a quiet state. All at once, I find myself down underneath the greens, which tower over me! Paradoxically, I'm formless, yet somehow also concentrated down to a very small size. I can feel the friendly unseen presences of Nature entities around me, yet am still aware of my physical body. I get a "Welcome to our world" kind of feeling from this lovely moment of communion.

The great gardener, horticulturalist, and botanist Luther Burbank (1849-1926) developed more than eight hundred new varieties of plants. Acutely observing and lovingly working with Nature, Burbank integrated his intuition with scientific experimentation. In the following passage from a lecture, he describes his own brand of attunement:

> In pursuing the study of any of the universal and everlasting laws of nature, whether relating to the life, growth, structure and movements of a giant planet, the tiniest plant or of the psychological movements of the human brain, some conditions are necessary before we can become one of nature's interpreters or the creator of any valuable work for the world. Preconceived notions, dogmas and all personal prejudice and bias must be laid aside. Listen patiently, quietly and reverently to the lessons, one by one, which Mother Nature has to teach, shedding light on that which was before a mystery, so that all who will, may see and know. She conveys her truths only to those who are passive and receptive. Accepting these truths as suggested, wherever they may lead, then we have the whole universe in harmony with us. At last man has found a solid foundation for science, having discovered that he is part of a universe which is eternally unstable in form, eternally immutable in substance.

R. Ogilvie Crombie, who was closely associated with the Findhorn Community, has written about the qualities required for well-attuned gardeners. In the posthumously-published book Meeting Fairies: My Remarkable Encounters with Nature Spirits, he shares the following message from the very heart of Nature:

> Special qualities are love of the earth and all vegetation; love of the work that has to be done; a determination to respect the earth and all growing things and to refrain from using chemicals and undue force to modify or alter the natural growth of plants, remembering that plants are

living things with a high degree of sensitivity; a total acceptance of the elemental kingdom and of the possibility of the success of the three-part cooperation which is one of the basic aims of the Findhorn Community. [*Ogilvie refers here to cooperation between devas, humans, and Nature spirits.*]...Those working in the garden must never forget that there are nature spirits of many kinds working with them, send love to them and give thanks for their cooperation.

Ogilvie, also known as "Roc" to his devoted friends at the Findhorn Community in Scotland, was one of the most refined and intellectually well rounded individuals I've ever known. I visited him at his book-lined apartment in Edinburgh, then travelled with him and a few other folks from the Findhorn Community to an eclectic spiritual conference at the late Sir George Trevelyn's adult education college at Attingham Park in England. When we said goodbye there, Roc gazed into me in a way that I have rarely experienced. It was a moment beyond time and space. I was directly touched and inspired by something that cannot be attributed to intellectual prowess alone in that moment: the undeniable blessing-power of a genuine spiritual adept.

Leslie and I met in 1970, just a few months after Roc and I parted. We've lived together since 1973, sharing many gardens and attunements to the devas and Nature spirits around us on our way to such a telepathic green communion as described above. We think along the same green lines! This poem celebrates our closeness to each other and to the Ozark bioregion where we live:

Birthday Poem For Leslie

When you came to live with me
many gardens ago
in the cabin by the lake
we began to watch waters
and sky slide by together
in Autumn's turquoise mirror,
and the heavens charged with rain.
Now the secret inscriptions of things
gradually appear to us-- written openly

147

in water and cloud, palm and eye,
feather and breath. The white star
flakes fall all night. The oak are there
all night to take them.
We are warm together under
our star-patterned portion of the quilt
of towns and breathing fields.
Here in our bed of seasons is
love.

"This is Deeply Dreamlike" (2011)

It's early April, and I drive up to Kansas City through the gathering greens to attend a family meeting. Before leaving, I sort through my mail and keep only a very short stack of items to be given further attention on return. One of these items is an invitation to a Buddhist Dzogchen meditation retreat led by my old teacher, Lama Surya Das. I'd done a month of silent retreats with him over a four year period, ending in 2000. We developed a fairly close connection, for which I was very grateful. I corresponded with him occasionally over the eleven years since I'd last seen him, but hadn't been quite moved to sign up for another retreat. So I save the invitation to consider later, not sure yet whether I want to actually address that recurrent urge to attend another retreat with Lama Surya Das.

I'm staying on the tenth floor of a hotel on the Plaza in Kansas City, right across the street from the Unity Temple. After two days of meetings, I wake one morning and stroll to the elevator to ride it down to the lobby prior to attending a last family conference. The elevator doors slide open, and a tall man stands there alone ohmygod it's Lama Surya Das! I'm absolutely mind-boggled by the synchronicity! He recognizes me quickly, and in the course of our conversation, invites me to attend a talk he's going to give that night at the Unity Temple, then to come as his guest to a day long meditation retreat to be held there on the following day.

As we walk through the hotel lobby together, I exclaim to Lama Surya Das, "This is deeply dreamlike." It's a Buddhist karmic comedy, a joyful and improbable reconnection. I do attend both his lecture and the retreat, and am refreshed by peace and silence. My wish for one more retreat with Lama Surya has been fulfilled; my meditative urge well met!

The Faery Feather (2011)

June sun presses its big hot thumb down on the concrete parking lot as I arrive at the Ozark Natural Foods Cooperative in Fayetteville, and back into a parking slot at the very edge of the shopping center. As I lock my car, I happen to see a large feather just behind it in a narrow perimeter area strewn with trash and tough, scrawny plants. Not wanting to unlock the car doors again, I pick the feather up and slip it through an open window. It wafts down to the front seat. I go into the co-op and shop, then head back toward my car with a bag of groceries. As I get about eight feet from my car, to my utter astonishment, the front door on the driver's side suddenly swings open, pauses for a moment as if to be witnessed, then closes itself firmly.

I reach the car, and try the door. It's locked!

I take the feather home, and place it on my altar, and later cleanse it with Peruvian palo santo wood, in much the same way that some people burn dried sage, sweetgrass, cedar, or juniper to "smudge" and purify a room, an object, or themselves.

Later still at twilight, I fit the feather into the slit end of a long wand of sycamore that's been stripped of bark and neatly gnawed by a beaver at the King's River.

Among animals, I feel a kinship with the Beaver Clan. Thus the beaver stick. The great Seneca medicine woman Twylah Nitsch once told me that in her tribe I'd be numbered among members of the Beaver Clan, because one of my keynotes is cooperation, embodied by beavers who build their dams together and live in colonies of nuclear family units, each family residing in its own lodge. Brandishing that fine-feathered beaver stick, I dance and celebrate the mystery of life and all its hidden kingdoms in the deep purple half-dark of dusk.

I wonder whether this mind-boggling event at the co-op has anything to do with earlier dreams and visions, and other more recent experiences with rings and buttons and sightings of small lights which have happened with some frequency in the first months of 2011. As I look back on these incidents, I ponder possible tie-ins with experiences I had in the nineteen seventies in Britain, and while making recent attunements in order to build collaborative relationships with local Nature spirits, and with the beings known to the Irish and the Scottish as the Sidhe, the ancient, evolved faery folk.

Just before the door-which-opened-and-closed itself, I'd become curious about the Sidhe. After reading the Celtic scholar John Matthews' account of his purported meetings with a representative of that distinguished line of subtle beings in The Sidhe: Wisdom from the Celtic Otherworld, I wanted to learn more about the history of human-faery interactions. In the days just prior to the enigmatic event at the co-op, I read a number of books that contain accounts by other supposed contactees, such as the Reverend Robert Kirk's extraordinary manuscript from the late 1600's, The Secret Commonwealth of Elves, Fauns and Faeries; W.Y. Evans-Wentz's huge, absorbing ethnographic collection of sightings, The Fairy Faith in Celtic Countries; selected books and essays by William Butler Yeats and his mystic Irish contemporary George Russell (aka A.E.); Eddie Lenihan's remarkable collection of recent faery sightings and interactions with humans in Ireland, Meeting the Other Crowd; and books by other modern authors who profess to have experience of the faery realm, including American author and mage Orion Foxwood, the spiritually gifted Scot R.J. Stewart, William Bloom, Brian Froud, and Signe Pike.

Perhaps all this reading opened me to a contact of my own, or at the least disposed me to a florid act of the imagination. At any rate, looking back now and connecting the dots... the very night before my weird experience in the parking lot, as I lie down to go to sleep, a rapturous, tingly feeling comes over me. It's so pleasant, I exclaim out loud, "I feel sooooo good," then rest back into a vibrant sense of well-being. The next thing I know, I feel a distinct presence enter my energy field and gently merge with my body-awareness. What I sense is friendly, but very Other, with both plantlike and human attributes; katydid green, greenleaf green, humming with life and brightly energized. For a minute more or less I feel doubled--a juxtaposition of myself and an uplifting yet serious masculine entity which seems like a diplomatic emissary from some parallel dimension of this Earth. Wonderment...

The next morning, when my car door swings open and closed at the co-op, I begin to suspect that the reverie of the previous night, and other earlier tokens of connection (such as finding the little button on my bathroom floor) might have been related, and led up to the moment when that door swung open, really grabbing my attention and confirming a genuine contact.

I am aware of our anthropomorphic tendency to personify subtle forces. Many people would be more comfortable with the notion that one might encounter *energies*, rather than actual *entities* of Nature. However, many others have reported sighting or sensing Nature spirits which seem to present themselves as described in venerable myths, or to mimic human behaviors, apparel, and habitations. This may be due solely to our own human projections, but it is also possible that these sentient energies "clothe" themselves in familiar forms for the sake of connecting with us in ways which we can relate to.

A day or two after the event at the co-op, a further synchronicity echoes and affirms my own experiences: I receive a journal in the mail from David Spangler in which he describes an unexpected contact he feels he has made quite recently with a member of the Sidhe. In his article, David writes:

> The contact with the Sidhe...has opened up new ways of thinking about the challenges that humanity is facing, and the help we are receiving...Contact with the Sidhe can be exciting for its own sake, but the deeper purpose behind what appears to be a new approach towards reconciliation is to break through the bubble that is forming around humanity due to the increasingly self-referential and human-centric attitudes and behaviors that characterize industrial and technological society...In this sense, the Sidhe become exemplars for us but not with the purpose of surrounding us with glamour or turning us away from our humanity. Rather it is to discover the larger, fuller humanity that can embrace both Sidhe and human beings and bring both into a new collaborative relationship. We need to break out of the human-centric bubble but not in a way that destroys or

151

disperses our humanity. Paradoxically, the Sidhe, by mirroring what a Gaian humanity might be like, can help us accomplish this.

(Quoted from David Spangler's <u>Views from the Borderland,</u> <u>An Esoteric Journal</u>, volume I, available by subscription from the Lorian Association, which publishes many other Spangler titles, as well as John Matthews' imaginative book <u>The Sidhe</u>.)

Looking Back

In 2010, I initiated a project which aims to marry scientific and psychic perspectives which might help us cope with climate change. My love for the earth moved me to jump into this and other environmentally related projects I've worked on over the decades, but I was also motivated by discouragement, fear, and grief. So many of us experience a sense of powerlessness and accompanying feelings of fear and despair concerning pollution and climate change. These feelings can either paralyze or catalyze us. In my own case, I've been less afflicted by sorrow as I've responded more proactively to the call to action contained within it. I pray daily to be a good magnet for the timing, contacts, information, and inspiration that will enable me to be an effective change agent for planetary well-being. We all can play a part in this endeavor, and every little bit helps. Though we could choose to see all our efforts as just a drop in the bucket, it's also true that buckets fill up drop by drop.

At the end of 2010, I came close to death due to a misdiagnosed illness which became a systemic infection. After returning home from a stay in the hospital early in 2011, I needed about a month to recuperate. For the first time in years, I had no appointments with clients. That precious unscheduled month became one of the happiest, most peaceful times of my life. While ill, I'd had to attune very closely to the needs and messages of my body. This capacity for more thoroughgoing attunement extended on into the year. I could sense how it amplified my openness to communications from nonphysical sources, which seemed to stream in more often as a result of my prayers to be of real assistance to Gaia. Some of the messages I received were subtle...an intuition; an improbable button found on the floor. Others were more dramatic...an impossible door-opening in a busy parking lot.

Most everyone who has had a close brush with death knows that it can help set our priorities straight and strengthen our commitment to whatever matters most to us. I committed myself to devoting more energy to collaborative environmental work, on the grassroots political level and as a subtle activist. I'd like to be both more subtle and more of an activist! However, these things build on themselves, and as my openness and trust have grown over this last period, so have the strength and coherency of that magnetic field I've been praying to manifest.

I'd like the stories in this chapter to help build readers' resolve to act on their own highest life priorities, and to trust more completely in the availability of spiritual alliances which can assist them.

"The Exchange of Living Energies"
(Looking Ahead)

I've shared many anomalous events in this memoir, with the intention of kindling an expanded vision of what is possible for us all. In <u>The Structure of Scientific Revolutions,</u> philosopher of science Thomas S. Kuhn points out that close observation of anomalies can lead to discoveries which challenge our established paradigms of understanding, and open us to new possibilities. When an anomaly is especially striking, some may even call it a miracle. Miracles can be challenging or inspiring, depending on one's point of view.

The burning of coal, oil, and gas has been a major cause of the ecological crisis. However, the Judeo-Christian paradigm of man's dominion over Nature has been an even more fundamental root cause. To survive as a species, we need new paradigms which evoke our caring cooperation with Gaia and the energies attendant upon Her, whether we think of these energies as devas and nature entities, or simply life-sustaining homeostatic forces.

In David Spangler's book <u>Facing the Future</u> (2010), he comments that

> ...miracles seem, well, miraculous to us because we don't understand the principles involved. But that doesn't mean we couldn't understand them. I believe that to do so, we need to approach them not as religious manifestations but as indicators of processes at work that are as natural in their sphere of operations as electromagnetism is in its.

David then references three instances of seemingly miraculous happenings, and continues:

> But in the three stories I told there is a clue that can start us down a path of understanding which I believe is germane to the power to face and shape the future. In all three cases, a relationship was involved, one that held and allowed for the exchange of living energies. In all three cases, as well, love was present in one form or another.

Love and relationship together make for dynamic collaboration. The "optimizing force" A.H. Almaas refers to can be observed in life's evolutionary impetus toward more complex interrelatedness and awareness. Nature is endlessly inventive and adaptive. As we mindfully "interbe" and lovingly interact with Nature, we can tap that inventiveness to discover new approaches to deal with the predicament of climate change. As we learn to attune to and work with other living energies on the planet, we may find that we can routinely do things that we would now regard as miraculous, to help harmonize ourselves and our societies with the environment.

As I see it, every moment is a natural miracle and each being is a boundless possibility. As William Blake wrote in The Marriage of Heaven and Hell (1793):

"How do you know but ev'ry Bird that cuts the airy way
Is an immense world of delight, clos'd by your senses five?"

Robert Sudlow wrote:

"The Kingdom of Heaven is spread across the earth--Now. Not in some future tense, not in the golden past, but now, eternally now. Awake."

And Dorothy Maclean wrote:

"When you're in tune with inner joyousness,
there is no
such thing as coincidence
or being in the wrong place.
What has been most mundane
is transformed and sparkles.
When you know this approach
miracles begin to happen around you
here and there and everywhere.
But you have to know it thoroughly, as something
quite practical."
[from The Living Silence, 1971]

We live in a country where all colors are sacred and alive. Here, there, and everywhere, *everything* brims over with its own unique Isness--not just extraordinary, non-ordinary phenomena. The following lines are from a song I wrote to celebrate this joyful mystery. You can hear me and my daughter Amy sing the whole thing at www geoffoelsner.com:

Ordinary Mystery

There's a line of silence on the land.
Silence reclines upon the land.
As day dips into darkness,
It'll widen and expand,
As primal silence settles on the land.

And that's an ordinary mystery,
An intricate simplicity,
A topsy turvy harmony,
A song that never ends.
Ordinary mystery,
Impermanent eternity,
Consigned to Time yet ever free,
My friend.

The mysteries and anomalies reported in these pages all hint at truer, healthier paradigms which could replace the prevailing, ailing ones of the past. They make a hopeful weave of meaning, suggesting that this world is far more responsive to our love and partnership than we have imagined.

More appreciations of this book...

"What a marvel of a book! Geoff Oelsner is himself such an empathic embodiment of the 'ordinary mysteries' he sings praises to throughout this remarkable ... I don't know what to call it...A shamanic memoir? A poetic 'Starry Night,' its electric golden energies shimmering through words instead of colors? An ancient mystic physician's bag of healing unguents, wrapped in straightforward recollections of his everyday life of serene, deep amazements? Thank you, Geoff, for this simple, sweet American Gaia Sutra."

– **Saniel Bonder**, Founder of Waking Down in Mutuality, co-founder of Human Sun Institute, author, *Ultimaya 1.0* and *Healing the Spirit/Matter Split*

"Everyone has times of transcendent and sacred experience, but most of us do not fully notice them. It is noticing and honoring that allows us to live the sacred as we journey through our lives. Geoff Oelsner takes us along on his kaleidoscopic travels in a way that heightens our awareness so that we may better perceive our own such experiences. *A Country Where All Colors Are Sacred and Alive* is a delightful vehicle of sacred wisdom of remarkable depth."

– **Anna Cox**, Founder of Compassion Works for All, which offers *Dharma Friends* newsletter for prisoners. Author of *Just As The Breeze Blows Through Moonlight*, and *Dharma Friends: No One Forgotten, No One Abandoned, No One Discarded*

CPSIA information can be obtained at www.ICGtesting.com
Printed in the USA
LVOW070605120412

277167LV00002B/6/P